# *The Spiritual*

# survival

## Guidebook / Handbook

Energetic Spirit life is a spiritual kingdom activity.
(Dealing with energetic spirit life activity from other worlds.)

A SPIRITUAL KINGDOM PERSPECTIVE SERIES

*AuthorHouse™*
*1663 Liberty Drive*
*Bloomington, IN 47403*
*www.authorhouse.com*
*Phone: 1 (800) 839-8640*

*Published by AuthorHouse  04/12/2017*

*ISBN: 978-1-5246-2149-0 (sc)*
*ISBN: 978-1-5246-2148-3 (e)*

*Library of Congress Control Number: 2016912286*

*Print information available on the last page.*

*Any people depicted in stock imagery provided by Thinkstock are models,*
*and such images are being used for illustrative purposes only.*
*Certain stock imagery © Thinkstock.*

*This book is printed on acid-free paper.*

*Scripture quotations marked KJV are from the Holy Bible, King James Version (Authorized Version). First published in 1611. Quoted from the KJV Classic Reference Bible, Copyright © 1983 by The Zondervan Corporation.*

# Table of Contents

# Dedication

**Dear Pastors in America,** as I pondered before the Lord whether or not I was done with this writing, suddenly I began to feel and sense deeply, that "Your prayers have touched, deeply touched the *heart* of God."
Thank you!

# To Jesus Sovereignty

Sovereignty meaning: jurisdiction, rule, kingship, supremacy, dominion, power (supremacy of power or rank), ascendancy, authority (having supreme authority), control(that all things are under God's rule and control), influence, unlimited power.....working all things according to His counsel. Eph 1.11.

To grandfather and mother, dad, mom, sisters and brothers and children, thank you for allowing me the time needed to complete this assignment. I sort of felt like Joseph who was taken away for a season, but I am still here; watching over you in prayer. Thank you for your prayers and doing life with me. May our family legacy of faith and heartfelt service to the Lord continue for generations to come until the Lord returns! Blessed be the name of the Lord, Exalted!

*Neal*

What a gift you are!. Peter 4.10. Our world is in need of your gift and God's grace upon your life. Surely, the world should meet you. So, OK world, meet Neal! A man that is truly gifted not only in business matters, but also able to genuinely care for others. He is also able to bring balance to people's lives, whatever situation they find themselves in, he is able to stabilize people with a sense that Christ is among us. He is an awesome organizer. A gifted "peacemaker" among men (thank you Jesus), of which the bible teaches:

### Blessed are the peacemakers for they shall be called the sons of God!

Rom 12.4-8
Ps.85.10
Corin. 12.27-28
Eph. 4.11-16.Matt. 5.9

Thank you.

# Introduction

Scripture says there is nothing new under the sun. Ecc. 1.9. When the people saw what Paul had done, the people lifted up their voices saying …

The **gods** are come down to us *in the likeness of men*. Act 14.11.

If the people recognized in Paul's days that the gods had come down, surely we are able to recognize that the gods have come down again and are operating among us, but for different reasons than they did in Paul's days.

chapter 1

# Processes of Various Aliens' Influences

How <u>other worldly beings</u> are connecting and in many cases have connected to our earth realm using many creative ways to attach to its inhabitants, seemingly to initiate and/or force its agenda in the United States:

- First by deception…Ps. 35.20. Prov. 12.20. Jn 1.7&10. 2 Tim 3.13.
 Acts 13.10. 2 Pet 2.13.
 - By first infiltrating our army systems … Ps. 2-3.
 - Now trying to press forward their agenda in our homes (families), churches, community (Policing and security systems), marketplace and all of society! … **Lead us again, O Lord**, those whom you have redeemed, we pray … For You are a man of war … Exo 15.3,9-13.

It seems that  the aliens first work was to do experimentation (using our cattle first, then humans), as spoken of by Anthropologist, on the History channel, now on DVD <u>Ancient Aliens</u> – Season 6, Vol. 2; but after their experimentation the alien beings found we were compatible with them to help breed **their** offspring, and now they plan to stay, but at our expense! As an entry point the aliens wanted to exchange information with our scientists and our army (the aliens were negotiating with us with a hidden agenda). More closer to the truth as a species, <u>the aliens were becoming extinct</u>. This reminds me of the bible story about David's enemies, who came to him for help, clothed in rags and looking destitute and *David did not check first with God*, but made a covenant to protect them, only to find out later, they were not who they said they were! Joshua 9.

**"You know them by their fruit"**, was the first thing I heard as I wondered how to begin this writing. Mt 7.17-18. Whether this fruit is initiated from the invisible or visible realm, doesn't seem to be the real issue because <u>if something is going on concerning you</u>, whether in the visible or invisible it <u>will</u> manifest. Cor. 4.5. It is a principle.

Even with all of the spiritual confusion being sent our way, by way of **research and firsthand experience**, we have found that the alien beings operating among us <u>can</u> effect the individual body, soul and mind in profound ways by a series of energetic spirit penetrating intrusions with intent (from the invisible realm), as well as a person's psyche (mind abilities).  1Co. 14.33.

What we need to understand is that fruit (bad fruit/a.k.a. energy/energetic fruit activity) can be energetically forced into a person's life (through their body's entry points) by other worldly beings (whether the initiation is visible or not, desired or not, is not a perquisite) Mt. 12.33 … we also need to understand and we have found that invisible other worldly beings can also force (its energy into a person's aura realm and/or by other  bodies surrounding its subject, by persistent spirit intrusion at different entry points on the body) into a person's physical and/or spiritual realm, energetically, until the subject's body is no longer the person, but the intruding spirit energy acting out, in the area being effected! K 4.1. Mk 5.13. Lk 8.30. Lk 8.33. Lk 22.3. Lk. 13.27.

As it was (in the bible days), and still is  another reason for the intrusion, because beings are, desiring a body to express itself in the earth. Rev 16.10., Lk.22.3. Dan, Rev 2.24-29. Ecc 3.1. Jude 1.9. I believe I am discovering that alien beings cannot thrive here (in our  realm) without some type of attachment to the body. Some may call it a parasite attachment (or intrusion for nourishment). They try to make the initial attachment quietly (first by  energetically penetrating their subjects spirit aura realm), once this is done it seems the beings will gain the ability to its subject vocal cords if certain conditions are right in the environment (like other energies in alliance, within a body within the environment; visible, or  invisible is not an issue), from here they have to energetically dig a bit deeper into the soul to gain the ability to  use its subject's character or personality. Energies have their own conscious personalities (ask Judas), if not they will war for this initial place also. A place they search for on the body, and it can explain why some people greatly effected by energetic energy will just seem to look at different places on the body (those operating through a person's life sometimes look for openings) – a place where other energies have penetrated, or spiritually energetically intruded upon in those they meet.

Depending on the assignment against the subject, another goal (initiative) is to get into the person's cell system. All matter has some level of cells, <u>and matter is anything that takes up space.</u> Then <u>begins</u> physical deterioration of the body. Wherever they are able to attach to the body, they will continue to war for the whole body, piece by piece; by it's energy coming into or upon that place. And then use these souls to attach to either family or randomly to others in the subjects area of influence in church and/or community. Sometimes in order to deal with the humans in Christ that understand how to resist alien being activity, the beings will literally cause some type of accident, and then, through the pain or confusion, the beings will slip in. It is another form of deception.

As a matter of fact, as things begin to unfold, it seems the aliens among us use penetrated spirit energy upon their subject (consistently-realized or not) until it first breaks through their spirit/ethereal realm, until it penetrates the physical body, and when the subject begins to feel the pain is when the alien realizes that it has made contact with the subject. And now the alien beings or energetic beings are ready for their next stage of processing its subject. See the pictures located at the end of this writing on how the being initially made contact with my life, intruding through time and space, the alien would begin to try to pull me into his reality. How, by the aches and pains the beings are able to cause by a process of excessive spirit activity upon one's energy field, and then contact is made into the body and soul, which was how I began to discover the reason for their intrusion!

The next stage would be to send its subject through a series of spirit penetrating energetic episodes evidently (seeming to either get its subject to do or not do something, a method to reveal its mastery upon the body and soul to inflect pain and/or aches _perhaps many would get stuck here and buckle or submit to the darkness under the pain or ache pressure)_. This would be the beings method of communication along with mind scan type activity thinking, and/or an actual meddling into its subjects mind, even trying at times to project its thoughts onto the subject. At Corinthians, 6.12; Paul said, I will not be brought under the power of any. 2Tim 2.26. This is where meditating on God's word (which is life or energy), to resist thoughts that try to become yours, but are clearly being sent to cause confusion. Jn.6.

With seemingly no way out (for the subject), the alien being would begin to energetically follow its subject throughout its daily schedule of activities, learning the lifestyle of its subject, while continuing to inflict spirit penetrations (causing spiritual distress or pressure that will eventually effect the body), energetically to let its subject know and realize that this being is not only follow-ing them, but is also continually causing the spirit energy and body distress that will eventually become a pattern, and/or daily ritual, while the alien being is also observing to see if its subject is going to submit to their intentions (of the thoughts they communicate to their subject) and/or resist it. This type of **_excessive_** spiritual activity will last as long as it takes for the alien being to get its message to its subject, that it did not come to visit, but to take over their subjects life, and/or actually if they can, trade places with its subject (in the subjects area of influence, whenever it wills – 2Tim 2.26) and in this way the other worldly being will make known its intention, whether its subject is being forced to submit or by forced alliance. Sometimes the beings will try to use others yielded to them to help the being finds its "place" in its subjects life. Eph. 4.27.

An example of a minister, by whom an alien being seemingly took over his TV-ministry, whose picture is listed at the end of this writing, even now, Peter Popoff, is on BET network (year of 2015).

Supposedly, when the entity leaves the minister at any time, the entity spirit being will assign another energy to guard and use (or misuse) the minister's body. The entity can use the ministers program to magically and or prophetically draw viewers, who will eventually become the new subject victim. Whether viewing the program or not, any potential viewer can be drawn to a commercial; to prophetically ensnare a potential subject victim, as well as others, even to support the show. Anyone should question why they would watch or support this show, in any way, especially those it seems to be drawing from a black network.

> Especially, when it seems the aliens have an agenda, regarding the black culture experiences, where a light culture would negatively connect with a church in Charleston, South Carolina; and the growing police civil infractions in the black community, both tend to be alien agendas. It is their DNA signature of other ways they are effecting our society, some of which is to cause distraction and division using deceit. And so, we need to look at the bigger picture. Joyce Meyer made a comment on a radio program, that aired in Columbus, Ohio, "you can't win a battle that you are pretending does not exist!"

Potentially, the entity can view you, then revisit you at night to begin energetically processing negatively, and you would not realize how or why you're being energetically attacked or effected in this way.

Another minister whose soul has been tremendously effected by consistent negative energetic intrusions, whose congregation turned him over to the Akron Beacon Journal, writer Bob Dyer, whose interview was commented on by the Washington Post internet article (regarding the Reverend Ernest Angley's megachurch), which made the following comments evolving Ernest Angley:

> - The illness plaguing Angley's empire, is Angley himself
> - Accused of tearing families apart
> - Pressures congregants to get abortions, vasectomies and
>   turn a blind eye to sexual abuse within the congregation

The former associate pastor, who resigned July 4, 2015, said Angley touched him inappropriately for 7 years. The former associate pastor, Miller, was told that the touching was a special anointing.

> I remember reading about an author who said, of the various types of activity that is supposed to be spiritual, that we, many churches and communities, as well as many in the world, do not seem to have a BS meter on spiritual activity, inviting and/or allowing anything that is spiritually initiated.

Other pastors, former followers said that the extent of control Angley had in the church ran deep and is now called a cult by many former members.

Angley stated in the article that the "devil" himself (as an energetic activity) has infiltrated the church, and Angley, (who is a prophet of God) has been working tirelessly to fight him off. www.akronbeaconjournalearnestangley.

Out of all that was said of Angley, I only found one note or resemblance of compassion, where, at the end of one of the internet articles, a woman said that she had visited Angley's church in the

1990's for prayer, and remembered that this man was anointed by the hand of God, and she said she'll never forget it! www.wksunews;akronbeaconjournalchurchabuse.com

I listened to a Moody radio program, that aired August 13, 2015, at 2.30 pm, where Tony Evans had spoken on the church's need to help restore others. This program caused me to wonder if anyone tried to restore Reverend Angley or even Jim Jones for that matter. These ministers did not need their church matter aired in a uncompassionate way, they needed restoration. These men were energetically warred against spiritually bigtime, even in many of the ways listed in this writing, their lives energetically afflicted day after day, night after night. Was it too much (their battling) for anyone to be considered able to help them, or help protect them from negative entities (energetic beings) who seemingly demanded their lives (continually) in warfare waged. This is a spiritual kingdom activity and there are only 2 spiritual kingdoms operating among us.

How often do these spiritual tragedies have to happen for us (the church and many in the world) to understand, or even recognize how important it is to deal more effectively, more intelligently in teaching the reality of energetic spiritual warfare tactics as preventative ways to help people not be taken by surprise? We may need to consider easier avenues for those gifted to help come along, to share and reveal how the Lord is able to lead us through times of energetic battling. It seems, those gifted trying to reveal what they know, have to first survive the personal energetic battling against them, the gifted, in order to gain the ability to help keep people out of the dark energetic activity that would operate against our society (one person at a time). Negative spirit energies seek the souls of men. Pet. 5.8. It seems we can't always work through conventional or accepted church ways, when negative energy is able to work against the church to the point of hindering the help that leaders may need to make it through. We need to operate more intelligently as a church, community, and as a society (in our gifting) … why should only dark intelligence seem to work more effectively among us? As a society, I wonder if we are operating with a full deck, with all cards on the table that are needed to teach all of what we are dealing with, and how to deal with what is engaging us from the spiritual realm (energetically) to effect us physically. *Where is our (spiritual) intelligence!* It seems God thinks we can do better!

How can anyone get help to the church, because they may have part of the answer, even if not known; or would they end up in jail or stoned for trespassing; because the church can't receive a gift unless everyone goes through their church protocol, and/or taught the ways of the church? Corin. 13.9. Jn.14.26. Did it work for Reverends Angley or Jim Jones?

> Some dark spirited energetic kingdoms cause some
> men's burdens to be heavy and grievous. Mt. 23.4-12.
> There is a need to learn how to bear some of the potential
> burdens that can happen being caused by spiritual
> energetic beings (and like these of what we are hearing
> of in the news) Gal. 6.2. Exo. 17.11-12.

Angley stated that the devil himself has infiltrated the church, and because this can occur, a church may need to go outside itself and actually look for the gift that is needed to guard them from the plots of any negative energies assigned to it, simply because the negative energy can be very deceitfully influential, especially if people are not being taught how to release (or cleanse) themselves from negative energies that have the ability to operate contagiously in any group and/or community, as well as church setting. Anyone who has a spirit and soul should be concerned with ongoing repentance and spiritual biblical cleansing and/or release. Why? Simply because dark spirit energetic activity (or developed spiritual energies) are always seeking to capture the souls and spirit-lives of men, from generation to generation. Pet. 5.8. Scripture teaches that this idea is not for any one culture or group, but those souls desiring to be and stay free from dark spirited energetic activity. *This is not a religious thing as much as it is protection for one's soul, and protection from spiritual invasion* from being forced into serving arrogant type spirit energies, or entities, developmentally negatively spirit energies. And so we pray for: cleansing from secret or otherwise faults, Ps. 19.2. Ps. 51.2. cleanse us through your word (your light, your energy ... ) Eph 5.26 Lord, help us cleanse ourselves from all filthiness of flesh and spirit, perfecting holiness in the fear of the Lord, 2Corin 7.1. So teach, teach, teach ... find help, find help, find help ... pray ... pray ... pray in Jesus name. Simply because doing nothing does not seem to work for us. I heard a minister say, "you can't win a battle that you pretend isn't there!" Why were there no ministerial safeguards, nor understanding of energetic extremes being used to capture souls (and the spiritual lives of men), for these ministers?

Many seemed (especially in the world) to point to these two ministers, as if they were in their right mind; however, from what I can see is that there is a need for ministers, in or outside the church, to learn how to protect themselves from developed worldly spirit energies that may come in deceit. Jn. 10.10. Rev 12.12.

*\*There* is a point of no return, when a minister allows (due to no help realized) or is taken by spirit alien energies to continually penetrate their life until it is truly *no longer* the individual and/ or ministers'. It is here that these ministers would appear to behave out of biblical character; and functions with an alien spirit being's agenda. There goes another minister that publically gets a bad rap due to spiritual overtake and/or ignorance, designed by developed spiritual alien intention and intrusion. And people say, "it don't take all that". Yes it does, it takes whatever it takes to get the "God" knowledge that keeps people from perishing before their time. A lot of people do not understand and would think, the minister is still a servant of God, but it's like the alien took over his ministry, his area of influence, his mind, soul and body through a process of hostile spirit intrusions; spiritually violating visitations and energy penetration activity, with the energetic intent to bring any servant of God into captivity (2Tim 2.26), and so people say it is God's minister; but (biblically) not really. I heard one writer say that we do not have spiritual BS meter. People are not understanding spiritual kingdom activity as it pertains to the only two spiritual kingdoms operating among us. Rom 14.17. Rev 16.

We need to teach more, like how the word of God is spirit (energy) and life. Jn. 6.63. People are not being taught how to release themselves from negative energies that evidently can effect their body, soul and spirit-life. Ask Ernest Angley and Jim Jones. Negative spirit energy intentions seem to bet on being able to accumulate their energy in the area of our lives that they are seeking to attach to and effect (to gain the ability to come through). How can we  teach what we do not know, nor understand. *People need to understand the importance of biblical and spiritual discernment*, because the difference will cause you to operate in either one spiritual kingdom or the other. There are only two spiritual kingdoms operating among us, only two! Our churches and our world need to understand that we are where we are because there is room for better understanding of these two ideas, that mainstream schools nor churches teach. What good is a education, if someone can come along and be used by darkness to knock you and your education out of commission, spiritually remove you through an ill-energetic process of filling you with negative energy and then cause you to do everything you never thought, as negative energy wills, because these are some of what is happening among us; realized or not does not seem to stop negative intentions concerning us (but offers a type of safe place for the dark spirit activity), whereas resisting these negative energetic intrusions would. Eze 22.26. Tim 2.26. *Wouldn't you want to know more about how spiritual energetic activity works?*

This writing does not necessarily speak to those already effected and do not realize it, and/or that are ok with this level of dark spirit activity and don't seem to mind being used by dark negative energetic spirit influence to effect others. This is the deception. These we are encouraged to pray for. 2Tim 2.26. Ps. 28.5. Thess. 5.23. Tim. 2.8. Except Gal 5. 2Tim 3.13.

You know them by their fruit....Mt.12

God does not operate against Himself (or against His word, nor does He operate against His Spirit character). Love and grace should be in your spirit-life activity and nature, if there is a struggle, this is where release or cleansing may be needed, because scripture says the Lord created us in his image. Isa 5.12. Heb. 13.15. Col. 1.8. Rom. 8.29. Gal. 5. 1Jn 4.8.

We fight the good fight of faith. We fight for love. We fight for a good life. We fight for justice. Arise, America and fight the good fight of faith! IJN!

There is no confusion in the Lord's ministry. It is honorable. It is excellent. 2Corin. 8.21. Yet scripture says "my people perish for lack of knowledge!" Hosea 4.6. This ministers mind, body and soul, was taken right in front our eyes. Just like the incident with the minister in Guyana, Africa. Spiritual alien energies are able to either take the minister's mind and/or their body. Whereas we all need a better understanding of energetic spirit activity because this minister probably needed help, but there was no one. Evidently! Just like the aliens spirit beings (through spiritual intruding visitations) are taking people now, penetrating them day by day, night by night, until the person needing help literally disappears in front of our eyes; their soul no longer there; no longer sound enough to ask for help. And then we allow the aliens to make the prophets crazy or insignificant, and they are in the foundation of God's kingdom. Where is everyone's help? What kind of energetic intelligence is this going on among us? Where is our spiritual intelligence?

God thinks (biblically thinks) we can do better! We are supposed to resist the enemy! James 4.7. We are supposed to rule in the midst of our enemies. Ps.110. But, who has ears to hear? Who is sound enough; humble enough to hear? Where are all the gifts the Lord is sending through so we can see our way? Or, are we too effected (energetically spiritually effected) to notice, and can we tell or are we past the point of recognizing. Where are the real sufferers?

In His light shall we see light … Ps 36.9

Are the alien spirit energies trying to sit on those the Lord is trying to get his revelations through, could you tell. Mt.16.17-18. Does the king need to throw a banquet to invite all the gifts, so that we can see He is good, and that He has already provided. How do we clear up this spiritual fog that the developed negative spirit alien energies have and continue to create among us?

Once these beings find a subject among us (this means the subject was first observed … Jere. 20.10), and locks them into a ritualistic format so to speak, then the being will proceed in the subjects family, and perhaps those who its subject usually does business with, in an attempt to **forge** itself into every area of its subjects life <u>in an arrogant/perverse manner</u>, tries to force a position of "god" in every area of its subjects life, and will begin to intrude in the subject's business matters to make sure everyone complies favorably to its subject (which potentially can cause the immature and/or the biblically unlearned person) to think, this god thing is ok (a type of flesh attitude), because they seem to be getting everything they want, and is another reason why we pray for everyone; because what we do potentially can effect others, as well, including the alien spirit agreements that we made. Gal. 5.12-13. <u>www.thecomingofficialannouncementofthealien.com</u>. <u>www.thegreadytreaty-youtube.com</u>. <u>www.retiredofficialdiscloseshuman-alieninteraction.com</u>. Some family members will be challenged or chosen over those who seemingly have no problem with the alien spirit beings agenda (however, this only seems to reveal a non-biblical level of understanding). Some who object (or resist in any way) will find they are sick often, heal very slowly, or face untimely death, unless we learn how to effectively resist the alien beings ill energetic initiatives for those it is sifting in the family or among us. Lk. 22.31. There are no accidents regarding any energetic alien spirit realm activity and connection to its subject, or operations happening among us. Job 4.16. Job 1.8 & 12.

If the internet links above have closed, simply do a word search in the address box until you find what's needed.

chapter 2

# The Possibilities and Potential Effects of Excess Spirit Energy on Humanity

Spirit energy (excess to excessive energy) that does not come necessarily consistently by way of seeking the Lord (and that seems to operate independently from the biblical ways of the Lord) could eventually change ones energetic spirit nature, if there is no resistance. Any excessive series of excess energy coming at you will eventually reveal its purpose by the outcome derived thereby. Lk. 12.2. NKJV. Skeptics may ask, do spirit energies really effect the body and why? Well for now let's just say Moses had to be protected from excess spirit energy activity desiring his body according to Jude 1.9. And the bible does teach that it is not good for a man to be without knowledge. Prov. 19.2.

It can be very interesting that so many people are on different levels of spirit energy activity; some are or have become advanced in their knowledge by efforts and ill intentions of negative spirit energies ability to pull anyone they seemingly choose into their arena or spiritual energy realm of activity, which is a dark energetic realm (with this realm comes a certain level of knowledge), at the same time these ill-spirit energies can isolate the subject from others, simply by causing others neither to hear nor notice anyone under their energetic intrusive influence. The other extreme is when the negative energies will cause others to speak on a subject's area of intrusion, without realizing they are speaking on a serious concern that is actually being experienced by the subject. How do we minister to someone without embracing them and/or, if ill-spirit energies are causing the majority to resist the subject, those that once were lovingly embraced. Mk 5.5.

## _How physical and/or mental symptoms and/or conditions due to excessive energy can arise to effect and connect in the following areas._

**- Head neck system function**(S) are directly influenced by the brain. The head and neck involves the brain, bones, muscles, blood vessels, nerves, glands, eyes, ears, brows, nose, mouth, teeth, tongue and throat. Movements are for chewing, swallowing and speech ...*

*The mind will be looked at below after this section of categories or more for depth in writing. For now, **I cannot stress enough** how important it is to resist whatever excess spirit energy activity would try to consistently affect your head.

Excessive radiating, gestating and or spirit energy penetration in this area can cause: discomfort, headache, and soreness, dizziness and stiffness, loss of memory (forgetting), faintness, neck ache, stiffness, pain, cramping, disorganization, and confusion. Sometimes these beings will test their ability, meaning they can penetrate your neck until it gets stiff, then they actually try to get you into a certain position (by a series of irritating contacts to the skin-which can feel like spirit burns) to get you to move quickly, so as to try to snap the neck. This is why it is preferred that once you sense anything energetic-wise, happening to your body try to offset whatever is happening to help bring immediate relief, until what seemed like what could happen didn't, because you responded to initial sign of subtle spirit energy intruding activity (including any heating sessions) and/or other energetic spirit frustrations.

Energy coming upon the hair, can be made to feel heavy on your head. Yes, excess spirit energy can rest on each strand of your hair causing your head to feel weighed down. Excessive spirit energy, consistently targeting or aimed at the head, could cause a tightness type of sensation, almost as if your head can't breathe, and prolonged energy seemingly resting upon the hair and/or head can cause dizziness and overall deterioration of brain function without resistance. Energetic spirit beings with an agenda have the potential to follow you around, while continually energetically penetrating your head (or vertigo) until you fell light headed; if this occurs it's best to carry vinegar spray and spray around your head as you walk, so the penetration doesn't cause you to be light-headed. When the lightness lifts while you are spraying, you will realize that you were dealing with something happening from within your environment. Also, water in a spray bottle alone may work for you. The goal is, of course, to stop the ill-spirit energetic flow upon the head (or hair). Excess spirit energy consistently aimed at the head is never a good intention and actually seems to thin the skin on the head (over time) to the point a head wrap (or thick cap) is necessary. This level of spirit penetration will also cause you to feel any temperature changes to be more irritating than refreshing. As time goes on, it will take less and less time for you to sense when any negative energy would begin to manifest in this area, because they can potentially cause a disorder and/or create new pathways in the brain (if not stopped), as places to lodge in your head from a series of day to day excess spirit energy, that is, without any resistance on your part. Some energetic beings will literally come into your environment just to penetrate your head. This is another way you could tell there

could be an energetic spirit assignment concerning you. **Whenever** you sense your head is being penetrated, spray vinegar, water and peppermint and water spray (or either combination, then wash your head in water as soon as possible), or spray around your head and/or wash your head continually *until you feel the penetration lift*, then you can know for sure there is a spirit energetic being in the environment causing the *energetic drama*. Sometimes light spraying will suffice, other times, more aggressive spraying will be necessary! Even soaking paper towels with hazel witch and/or vinegar and water, then place on the head and wrap with a towel can also bring relief.

Some various level energetic beings, as an assignment will seem to sit in the head and you can actually feel them sucking the protein from the scalp. Get them out as quickly as possible, with the above methods or sometimes just wiping shampoo on the head and letting it sit a bit then wash it out. But if these beings come in the night and you are really tired, listen don't hesitate to put gobs of peanut butter in the head and then wrap the head! This could buy you a couple of hours of sleep. Then rinse out upon waking. Sometimes the beings will suck the peanut butter dry and the dryness will wake you. It's ok, wash out peanut butter quickly, then apply some more, wrap, then back to sleep. Daniel 7.25.

The bible teaches that spiritual things can be perceived, as Job perceived something was causing the hair to rise on his body.

**... Then a spirit passed by my face, the hair of my flesh stood up** – Job 4.15.

Prevent possible head issues when the above signs or spirit energy activity occurs by keeping the neck and/or head washed up, soaking these areas if needed _until the energy lifts_; this would depend on how much energy is coming to you at one sitting (or intruding) session, or seemingly more like a series of penetrating episodes. In the passing of time, if you notice a greater dose of energy coming upon this area (or one area of the head), you could add either witch hazel and/or a mixture of vinegar and water, the strength can be determined by how anxious the energy spirit beings are trying to accomplish their intrusion process into this area. The greater the intrusion then the greater the strength of vinegar/or witch hazel and water, plus peppermint, optional (can be added for a different smell and stronger effect). At times you may find that peppermint extract alone can resolve a certain level of head intrusions, by putting the peppermint on a towel (or paper-towel) then rub either the whole head and/or wherever the energy is causing irritation. This is if, and until, you can get around a sink to wash your head. Sometimes in travel, the energy can seem to suddenly come spontaneously upon you, just wipe shampoo in the head until you get home, or pull to side of road if it is safe to do so or a rest area, and grab a couple of bottles of water to rise out the shampoo and you'll feel refreshed. So just keep rinsing out the energy with water _until the penetration stops_ and/or the discomfort lifts. Usually, a continual increase of energetic intrusions will also signify there is harm intended, and/or there is an energetic spirit assignment to affect that area.

> In extreme cases, where energetic spirit beings are penetrating the head day and night and your head skin may begin to wear thin, peanut butter could help protect your scalp, like a buffer from excess spirit energy being focused in this area. Even on an airplane one could seriously be energetically spirit attacked while everyone else seems OK.

It may be _a tedious process but it beats having open head surgery, or unwanted mental challenges_ that could occur from not resisting the negative energetic activity.

Please remember that we are dealing with intelligent, seemingly relentless beings, and if you are successful at keeping any excess energy accumulation off your head, they could try to penetrate your neck, as a method or strategy to affect your head. So check neck and, potentially, your ears often and keep them at a normal temperature as possible. Any extra devious excess spirit energy activity could also potentially try to slip into your mouth and/or your ears (as an acid type of spirit energy effect) to irritate. These areas should be kept wiped off and/or rinsed until the spirit energy lifts. These types of beings seemingly are trying to get you to go to the hospital, especially hospitals with employees that are energetically affected, who will literally try to keep you longer than necessary. We are dealing with an energetic ill-spirited kingdom operation. No offense hospitals, it is simply how they (energetic spirit beings) operate. We're seemingly all in this together and, therefore, everyone needs to better understand the energetic spirit activity operating among us!

**Diet** is important to this list of categories because excessive spirit energy targeting any area of the body _for steady lengths_ can potentially cause a nutritional and/or vitamin imbalance, and you would probably not even realize it due to the constant distraction energetic spirit penetrations can cause. Example, you could go to the hospital because you think your throat is sore, but really the excess spirit energy is also secretly depleting your energy to the point that normally you would have the energy to resist a sore throat, but not if the excess energy was affecting your immune system. Therefore, it is necessary to check to see if you are not being depleted of nutrition and vitamin intake on a regular basis, if energies are trying to operate in your life directly from the environment or those people that are being energetically forced into energetic spirit services. There is a reason these beings are trying to affect and ill-influence our nutritional health systems.

**Eyes:** Once a person's aura realm (and/or area around their body) has been energetically spirit penetrated enough, energetic beings are literally able to fly into the subjects eyes (or wherever they want to affect) and cause the eyes to seem to go cross-eyed (or seemingly haywire or wacky at will. 2Tim 2.26). Simply shut the eyes until one senses the activity has passed. Should it happen again, repeat the process. If it is safe, or if you are alone trying to concentrate on reading and this happens, spraying around and/or above you could also release you from this type of intrusive spirit energy activity. This spirit energy activity is simply letting you know that it is trying to find a place to operate in your life and/or environment. Biblically, we are not supposed to give it a place. James 4.7.

What is even more important, these energetic spirit beings are able to cause your eyes to look puffy because these beings are able to draw certain nutrients from the blood, which can directly affect the blood vessels under the eyes. When you sense this is being done, it can potentially cause you to feel faint. One solution is to keep a protein drink available, to quickly put any needed protein and other nutrients back, and literally to get your balance back!

**Goal:** *We must first gain the ability to **recognize and discern*** when these spirit energies start coming upon the head or neck, etc., and realize how long it seems to stay, and know that doing nothing does not work. We are dealing with a level of light beings (made of matter, meaning these energies are trying to take up space(s), not only in various areas of our lives, but also in our bodies) they not only look for places to attach, but that can also have the ability to create space in our bodies for themselves, at our expense. In other words, our pain (or discomfort) is their gain. The goal is to release this area from excess spirit energy, and not allow the energy to rest, soak or gestate in any areas of concern, due to the permanent damage it causes to the brain if they are able to attach themselves to, not only the scalp, but actually go into the cell system of the brain, and even create new pathways (and/or literally create types of disorders or malfunctions) in the brain, or simply go in and control that area (by their will) if the need to them arises. 2Tim. 2.26. As if you had a drawer and someone decided one day to rearrange everything. So how would you find your brain, if things seemed suddenly rearranged up there? You wouldn't. So perhaps it's better, due to the level of energetic spirit intrusions happening in our nation all around, to just resist any excess spirit energy trying to affect you. And please, don't forget to keep seeking the Lord's guidance, help, and wisdom through any energetic engagement concerning you. It's coming to you from a different realm and they are breaking though time and space to intrude. It is in the Lord, we live and breathe and have our spirit being and life in the earth. Acts 17.28KJV.

> This could feel like a lonely process for anyone to go through alone and a threat to one's existence. It would be great for someone (that is able to learn how to protect themselves in this area) to come and sit with such a person and help bear the burden. What is needed is a compassionate warrior in Christ. Not some one with no understanding and sympathy who could make the journey seem longer. Who would want a miserable comforter? Job 16.2. Also bringing this person to church would be kind, but you would need to stay with this person, if there is an assignment regarding this precious soul, the negative energies could potentially cause

trouble all around this soul, in order to isolate the person from community. If you could offer this type of friendship/fellowship only once a month, I am sure this person would be so very grateful. How are we able to teach unity in the community if we do not teach how to release one from the negative spirit energies operating among us? Often disharmony and disconnecting people from unity and community is happening in the work place, where many have been affected by negative spirit energetic activity that has manifested in ones home, then carried into the workplace. The Spiritual Root of the Matter is Found in Me might be helpful. Lord, help us to caringly bear one another's burdens, in Your Name!

Gal. 6.2 Bear one another's burdens and so fulfill the law of Christ!

- **Digestive system** (includes the gastrointestinal tract, and functions to; breaks down food into small molecules which then makes food absorbable).

  The digestive system is divided into 2 major parts;
  1. Major part is the alimentary canal and is continual
  2. Major part has 2 openings; the mouth and the anus; the liver and pancreas are also included in this system.
  www.humanalimentarycanal.com
  www.functionofdigestivesystem.com

Excessive spirit energy; Can come at any time, for any reason that may give rise to it, some of are mentioned in this writing. After the body has been penetrated enough (making way) so that whatever spirit energy is sent, assigned and/or in the territory, and initially, usually from a seated position, will come and just sit (or manifest itself) on ones bottom; sometimes one may feel the energy sit at certain parts of the bottom of one's hips, and seemingly hug the area that feels the warmest, from there it can rise up into the intestinal system and just begin to harden the stool as part of its expressed activity on and/or within the body and/or wherever the discomfort is found in the digestive system. We must remember that energies that consistently come to you have a personality, various levels of intelligence, and some energetic beings can be considered hostile and can cause diarrhea, *hemorrhoids,* and/or constipation sometimes every day, in these areas, if you allow it, and/or release is not found.

Anywhere spirit energies want to squeeze into, they seem to find a way using intrusive energetic spirit activities (as their expressions) to find access to your time as well as, the body, soul and spirit life. Potential remedy: There are drugstore remedies for diarrhea and/or constipation the energetic spirit activity can cause. You could also use vinegar on a towel (using the strength that works for you, mixed with water if desired) and simply sit on it when aggressive spirit energies try to aggravate this area, either right inside or directly outside the underwear is fine, until the *energy lifts*. Sometimes it may take a little time to address this issue, other times you may need to soak the bottom area to force the excess energy out, and there may be times you may fall asleep with this towel in place. It's ok, as long as it is wet it can keep out the intruder. If it dries while sleeping, the spirit energy could possibly return to awake you, as it seems to somehow think this could be home for them. www.thevinegaranniversarybook.com.

These are just some of the home remedy methods found helpful; in dealing with this matter, some may want to check with their doctor, and this is OK, especially if your doctor understands how energetic spirit activity operates among mankind as addressed in this writing; if not, other doctors are available, either way, this could keep you safe until the Lord reveals otherwise. Many have said we are our own best doctor. Again, this writing is just reaching out to those in need, and who may not have the money for a doctor, who may need to research on how energetic spirit activity can and is affecting many.

Also, while driving, have a towel available if spirit energies try to irritate your bottom with heating sessions through your seat area. These energetic spirit beings do not seem to value the things (like the cars) we pay good money for. Having a bag of ice to sit on may be helpful. Please write, if other solutions are needed, we would be able to offer other suggestions. This is only until the Lord brings complete healing to our nation, in Jesus, Amen.

Diet is important, fruit and/or water can help regulate your bowels during, or around, any spirit energy activity. If you have time for it, this is why I am mentioning other alternatives. Sometimes you may want, or need, to make sure the bowels stay undisturbed, if there seem to be consistent energetic spirit activity in this area, by either taking a laxative and/or anti-diarrhea pill to *offset* what negative spirit energies try to do … determined and/or revealed by the actual outcome they create and/or are able to cause. Exercise can also help to off-set how negative energetic activity could be trying to affect the body.

Excessive spirit energy that seems to go right for the acid reflux area; you can find almost instant release by sipping on coconut cooking oil, or oil of your choice, and/or water will take away the burning sensation. You can chase the coconut oil down with water. Again there may be other drug store remedies, found at local stores. Some doctors with knowledge and understanding can be helpful. Some doctors do not understand anything about  energetic spirit activity (that many can be hostile), as yet, and may want to put you on meds, perhaps as a new pathway that a doctor may be more familiar with, but that may not be as helpful as you think. Energetic beings are also found to work around meds, and attach to another area (and even are able to come through as a spirit altar in the soul) just to continue their expressions. It is an amazing thing happening among us, like its been a part of history waiting to be told.

It can be trying but please don't give up your faith in God's salvation through Jesus.
Hebrews 10.35

You don't have to be mental to deal with what is trying to engage you. All you need is an understanding of what you are really dealing with, and that these energetic spirit beings are able to pull just about anyone they want it seems (who is not aware of them or too spiritually affected by them), into their spirit reality – by their consistent illegal visitations. So we just need to learn how to be wise, regarding the matter. Joyce Meyer said in so many words, you can't win a battle you are pretending does not exist! It may be best to find a more understanding doctor, otherwise this is another good reason to log all energetic spirit intrusive activity, perhaps keep a note pad by the bed. Placing the day and time of activity at top of paper before going to bed could also prove helpful. However, given the different types of energetic spirit intrusions, sometimes it may not be possible to write as soon as one awakens, so remember what you can in the morning. Also, list any daily sudden sore areas and/or strange marks on the body that seem to come from nowhere.

It may be a good idea not to drink too much water especially at bedtime, as some energies like to run through your urine system, just like they like to run through your bowel system. Let's not get upset, just deal with the excess energy activity in Jesus name. Besides it is written, wrath works not the righteousness of God. James 1.20. Praying often can be very comforting to a believer. Prov. 13.6.

Some energetic spirit beings  can gain the ability to cause their subject to throw up their food, once the energetic spirit being has energetically processed that area of the body (through constant visitation in and/or around that area) which simply means the energetic being has trafficked that area (back and forth, back and forth, etc.,) until their goal is accomplished. If the subject *could learn to discern and recognize when the ill-energetic being is trafficking in this area, you could find ways to interrupt their process,* which would be ideal. Gargling water, or whatever works for you. I have used alka-seltzer and/or a mixture of vinegar, water and baking soda, and continue to sip and/or drink until you sense the area is cleared. Sometimes the being will lay low and then try later, so always be prepared to resist their intrusion. James 4.7. Mt. 24.13.

Sometimes the energies sent will change guards (as the energies operating in the earth seem to be ruled by the powers in heavenly places; Eph. 3.10). Yes, there seems to be someone directing their work, and it seems that if certain spirit energies are not causing any serious problems in the area that any one of them gravitates to, *then another one may come* and continue to work, not only in this area but wherever else; you can tell when other sudden body aches or issues seem to arise. *Exercise is important*, especially walking to help keep your muscles moving. Some spirit energy activity will rise or manifest when you try to get into your daily walking exercises with distractions that may hinder you from getting dressed, while you are trying to get ready, or even during walking, often strange physical and/or environmental distractions can even come from certain animals; dogs, fowls, mosquitoes, or nets that energetic spirit beings are also able to operate through as they will. 2Tim 2.26. That's ok, just don't let them bite you, patience is working also. Just find a spray that will keep them from pestering you; otherwise they can keep you swinging at them for hours. A vinegar and peppermint spray with water could also be helpful; and then let patience have its perfect work. James 1.4. Praise the Lord! We can still count our blessings. **We can pass through this together if people would just learn how to deal with the excess spirit energies we are being confronted with.**

**Spiritual Goal:** Allow patience to have its perfect work … for in your patience possess ye your souls … James 1.3, Lk. 21.19. Do not let the excessive energy gestate upon your bottom; it can lead to larger problems. These beings are able to keep your bottom heated every time you sit down. Depending on how anxious the beings are trying to bring harm, physical harm consistently until you either get the area checked out, or an unexpected emergency could arise from them making continual heated contact with your bottom. Some people they can, and will, potentially pester their bottom area from the  time the subject gets up until the time they lay down. If so, find a way to keep them from keeping that area heated and/or gestated with heat. One method could be to sit on a wet towel until the heat breaks or lifts, otherwise they could also cause problems from keeping this area dried out, to the point sores could develop and/or continual itching.

Prayer is also important. And the word of God is spirit and life (life is energy, energized by one's potential spirituality or energetic spirit devotion to Christ, to support your level of faith, coupled with time spent with the Lord). Jn. 6.633. The Lord who says call unto me and I will tell thee great things which you know not of. Jeremiah 33.3.

## Respiration system; supplies the blood with oxygen in order for the blood to deliver oxygen
to all parts of the body, and this is done through breathing or circulatory system. When breathing, we inhale oxygen and we exhale carbon dioxide. www.functionofrespirationsystem.com

Excessive spirit energy: Always watch for any consistent discomfort or sudden and/or steady subtle energy spirit penetrations upon the skin in any area where your blood could be affected. Sometimes simply shaking and/or exercise are potentially able to dislodge certain levels of excess spirit energy. Amen! Isa. 30.32. Also, verbally releasing this area in the name of Jesus consistently can also be an added effective way to help preserve your body, soul and spirit life in Christ. We have a flow chart with the Bible names and descriptions of Jesus authority to assist you, and you will find that the Lord is faithful.

## Endocrine system; is made up of a collection of glands that produce hormones that regulate
the body's growth and development (physical and chemical processes of the body), tissue function, reproduction, sleep, metabolism, and sexual development. The endocrine system also includes the pituitary, thyroid, parathyroid, and adrenal glands, pancreas, ovaries (for female and testicles for males). The word endocrine means within. Generally, a gland can select and remove materials from the blood process them and secrete the finished chemical substance or product anywhere needed in the body. www.merckmanual. www.functionofendoctrinesystem.com. Any physical and/or soul imbalances can also be due to imbalances or uneven levels of consistent excess spirit energy operating, and are able to effect any areas of this system.

Excessive spirit energy; the endocrine system can also be relational to (or be affected by) our chakra system, and excessive energy on the body could also potentially cause a chakra to become imbalanced and visa versa. www.chakraandtheendocrinesystem.com.  www.balanced-energy.com.

When dealing with areas of the body that are not easily accessible, don't forget **diet and prayer** become a continued priority for any of these categories. As I said earlier, constant excess spirit energy penetration in any area can cause a nutritional and vitamin imbalance in any endocrine area, including the blood. What must be learned, and then discerned, is when the energies are there, then resist and/or release yourself from their harm, naturally and spiritually so, in Jesus name. Also, we have a **_flowchart_** with a list of the names of Jesus to help with prayer support and releases in these areas, and it is also able to help ease any troubled mind and bring peace. A mind stayed on the Lord is kept in perfect peace. Isa. 26.3. I also need to mention that some levels of energetic activity are able to literally slip into your mouth, lodge in the throat or mucus area, and cause excessive coughing or other issues if not resisted. Sipping on coconut oil and/or a cough drop could prove helpful. Also, using a menthol rub on the neck ( like artic ice ) can also cause the energy to release the throat, or sometimes **finding** release can be as simple as gargling with water.

Please note: Catching any energetic spirit activity in progress (by resisting it) can help prevent potential side effects to the physical spiritual and soul system. _Please journalize these activities_.

Dealing with energetic spirit activity is a reality that can affect the body, soul, and spirit life <u>and is not just a mental idea</u> or development that comes out of the blue; therefore any physician care sought without this understanding can cause a potential misunderstanding, more symptomatic than a physician that understands those seriously affected by ill energetic alien spirit beings operating energetically among us.

**Spiritual Goal:** Do not allow the energy to continually or ritually gestate upon your body; the longer it is there opens an opportunity for any excess energy to be able to reach deeper and deeper into any area. Also, for any coughing seizes, if there is no cough medicine around, I would try to sip on some coconut oil (or oil of your choice) and then chase it with water, then repeat the process until you can find further relief if needed, as soon as possible, especially if coughing symptoms come suddenly, for no apparent reason.

<u>**Prayer is important:**</u> Lord, help us find doctors and nutritionists who can help your people offset any spiritual negative energy trying to affect the body and/or soul, and help these doctors and nutritionists make themselves available to your people, in Jesus name. Thank you.

- **Reproductive system** (organs and glands that aid in reproduction). The female function is to produce egg cells and then protect and nourish the offspring until birth. The male system is to produce and deposit sperm. www.functionofreproduction.com

Excessive spirit energy: I believe with all my heart that spiritual beings can interrupt any of these processes, to the degree that the spiritual energy beings are able to come and gestate this area <u>if there is no</u> sufficient resistance. Just this year (2015), we saw on the internet a woman who just had a baby and the baby did not have a nose, causing it to look physically alien. Was there an alien or spirit energetic intrusion in the womb trying to reproduce itself? Women, we need to become more intentional in protecting this area of our body's and soul life. Supporting websites: www.babybornwithnonose.com www.babybornwitheyeonforehead.com

Here in Africa, it says 50 deformed babies were born in the last 2 years and there is no documented cause for the growing trend. <u>Now there is</u>! Thank you Lord.

Plus, they say that our lower extremity area <u>is most often where cancer is found</u>. Is it a coincidence that these particular worldly spirit beings are often found operating in our nation; <u>love</u> this area also, and some spirit beings come religiously or ritually (daily) just to sit (or manifest) in the reproductive area (gestating wherever they can find a place); potentially causing mishaps and possible inflammation, etc., in these areas if there is no resistance. Some spiritual energetic activity can cause soreness, aches or pain in the ovaries and/or fallopian tubes, as if these spirit beings were a hotel room seemingly trying to make room for themselves, and by doing so can cause weakness in the area and potentially cause some level of removal, dysfunction and/or disintegration. Eph. 4.27.

We are beginning to realize that the alien spirit beings cannot seem to live nor exist in our realm, on a certain level of existence in our world, without attaching to (our physical bodies). And once these spirit beings find a place, from there (wherever they attach) they will begin to extract protein and other nutrients from the body, to sustain their lives and seeming agenda (using our lives and positions in life) at our expense. These beings can be released in prayer (even though they try to come. Lk 10.10). Also, there are certain medicated creams, such as <u>artic ice</u> that really moves them out to help keep them from gestating on any  area of your body, which in itself, over time can cause issues.

Yet, they can and do come back, and often do when one is asleep and/or preoccupied with daily activity. Everyone has to sleep, so what do you do? You continue to fight the good fight of faith while resisting what the energy spirit being is trying to do to your body and/or soul. You try to resist their *overall* intent for coming into the areas of the body and/or soul that seem to interest them (signified by the continual pain or ache or distress, etc., they can cause). I have even known of a person who actually used peanut butter to coat her bottom area to seal private parts from physical intrusion, and even though the spirit beings would try consistently to warm the bottom area, to melt and dry the peanut butter by the heat the spirit beings are able to generate, to gain entrance to do their bidding. However, the woman continued to use it to help <u>slow down the alien energetic spirit beings activity and intention and again protect herself from energetic spirit gestation</u>. I suppose any kind of seal buffer that is safe and effective would work.

Whenever the peanut butter would begin to melt or make the bloop, bloop sound indicating the energy had penetrated through, one would simply add more peanut butter, as it seemed to give a sense of peace in knowing that as long as she kept using the peanut butter she did not have to deal with the disgusted feeling of these spirit-beings running in and out of her private parts, as she continued to seek the Lord for complete relief because you can only sensibly deal with any excess energy issues with the greater and wiser source of energy. <u>God is Spirit</u>, Spirit is also energy, people. Jn. 6.63 "A sign of the times"! Jn. 4.24.

During the times of seemingly energetic distress, don't seek to commune with the energy (which can be considered demi-gods) causing the distress, seek the greater energy. The <u>only</u> Spirit God and highest energy. The only God that is able to offer salvation to men, through Jesus Christ our Lord. **God is a free Spirit.** A lot of people do not understand this, because *often* people's first introduction to any spirit god is some level (growing level) of spiritual captivity and/or bondage; people need to understand and realize where they are and structurally whose kingdom activity are they fitting into or being forced into.

**God's Spirit is good,** not the spiritual negative energetic activity that seeks to harm you by controlling your every move and intention. Alien being energies seemingly do not let its subject rest; they are very controlling by the nuisance they become (revealed in those they are able to energetically manifest through). This is another good reason to learn how to gain the ability to resist them, in Jesus name. A good place to start is repentance! Not just for us, but whoever the Lord brings to mind! It seems we're all in this together and we need to get it right (the important things in life, like learning how negative spirit energy can affect us, and then, through God, learn to offset and overcome them in Jesus name, Rom 8.37) simply because we seem to affect each other when we get things right or when we get things wrong. Jn. 6.63. Ps. 51.12. Corin. 8.13. Rom.14.21-22.

# Restore to me the joy of thy salvation, and uphold me with Thy
## *Free Spirit*

The woman that used the peanut butter found out that whenever the energy would penetrate the peanut butter it would run through her urine causing her to urinate excessively until it became clear that the energy was running through her urine system to deteriorate it. Similarly, this can be done with the bowel system. Likewise, this energetic method can be used to deteriorate any part of the body. So it is a good idea to keep excess spirit energy activity out as best you can. When you awake, and at night until they awake you trying to get in, reinforce your protection. You see when you can preserve your body's health, you can also help to preserve your soul. Thess. 5.23. Remember in scripture the woman in the synagogue who was bowed over. Lk. 13.11. Sometimes when the spiritual alien energies see that you are gaining the ability to protect your bottom and keep them out more often than not, they will get upset (they do have personalities, usually negative and bothersome) and try more aggressively to get to your bottom, as if it belonged to them (Acts 19.15-16); again get to a private place and make sure you have in your bag a bath towel, fold it, sit on it and use with water bottles, just begin to lift your hips to the side and pour the water under your seat to dilute the negative energetic intentions, until it lifts and/or until you can get to where you are going and then change into dry clothes!

Often negative spirit energies can become more assertive and will work overtime while you are driving, and you may need to pull off the road, pull into a quiet or inconspicuous place to deal with the energies, with padding or the fluids needed, so that they are not able to distract you as much while driving. Also, be sure you cover yourself while dealing with your issues because many business and community locations are using cameras to oversee parking lots, and will call the police and replay the tape for the policemen as a way or method of getting the police to remove you from their place of business. Doesn't seem to matter if you have an emergency whereby you may need to deal with any private concerns in the privacy of your vehicle. Doesn't seem to matter, <u>if you are a patron</u>! This is proving to be a real inconvenience to business patrons – as if they no longer needed customers. A sign of the times. Whether at a business or a park, after about 15 min., seemingly it is time to move on or police will be called and/or just show up. A real militant view continues to arise among us; but why the excessive camera viewing, as if they were looking for criminals at large continually? How then do you tell if there is an emergency?

If everyone that pulls into your parking lot is under criminal suspicion, if patrons are there for more than the allotted 15 minutes, if customers are treated as discourteous and/or as criminals?

Dan. 2.20. Ps. 104.24.

**Spiritual Goal:** Resist them. James 4.7. No matter how trying, it's less work than allowing them (energetic spirit beings) free reign continually because they never stop wanting to spiral you deeper and deeper into their reality and realm of excessive dark energetic spirit activity (beyond your will or resistance). Jn 10.10. I am coming to realize that these beings may need to attach to these areas just to survive as well; we are realizing that these beings are also able to deplete our nutritional and vitamin levels. **Diet is important. Prayer is important.** *Gal. 5.19-21 would be some of their activity.*

## - Hair/Skin system: (function to protect body's living tissue and organs, also protects against invasion by infection). It is important to learn to resist any daily energetic spirit heat treatment invasions to the head, as well as the skin.

Excessive spirit energy can affect this area also, again depending how free the energies are allowed to gestate upon the body. The negative spirit energies will usually effect the weakest part of the body and/or create a weak area of the body simply by manifesting heat continually in the area it is felt upon the body, with no resistance (wherever you sense energy coming in or going out) or they are able to create a weakness and/or dysfunction in the body through various constant excess spirit penetration sessions on or within your body's system. **Diet, exercise and prayer are important.** Depending on the personality of the energy, I have had them weigh so heavy on the hairs of my head until my head actually leaned to one side. So, I called on the name of the Lord, who said to me "wash your hair"! Praise the Lord. Jn.2.5. Acts 2.21.

Can we understand that some spirit energy will come to manifest, just to try to intimidate and/or to annoy, just like some of the people they have already affected or possess (and or/are able perhaps to annoy and/or intimidate, and is a way energetic spirit beings can express themselves through humans, they are able to attach to and/or work through, or seize in the environment for their service) and thereby people are revealing that help or release is needed? Prov. 28.18. Rom. 10.13. Acts 19. There are some higher levels of energetic spirit activity that are able to manifest upon the skin as rashes, just to get you to scratch from excessive itching, and cause various levels of irritation (or sores) and ultimately inflammation. Some levels of energetic spirit activity have the ability to puncture your skin, especially your hands and feet; they would try to get it to fester as an open wound, or even be the cause of inflammation (by simply expanding inside your shoe as one of their energetic spirit methods and/or manifesting a continual level of heat to the hands or feet) to cause you to either wear open shoes or, if the sore they create is on the hip area, it's to cause you to wear your clothes or shoes more loosely so they can have easier access to you. Keep hands protected with Vaseline and/or gloves, whichever becomes necessary. ***Keep skin cleansed and try to protect those areas that seem to interest them (energetic spirit activity that comes upon the skin) the most.*** There are drug store anti-itch creams and antibiotic creams to help prevent infection. Some beings can actually come upon you and cause you to instantly become warmer … until you literally come out of your clothes. Just start drinking water to pull that temperature down and you can also use ice packs. In this case, a fan may help, if getting naked is not your solution, nor appropriate. Fans could also prove helpful in hotels, *where many energetic spirit beings have the ability to collect.* It is useful for hotels, even lawyer offices, any office building and/or places where people gather, to use a Lysol spray when everyone leaves to <u>release</u> these areas from negative spirit energy collections. Those using Lysol, be sure to cover nose and mouth until you are in an area where the air is clear. If Lysol is too strong, peppermint mixed with water in a spray bottle can prove helpful. www.peppermintextractuses.com. www.miracleofpeppermintoil:20practicalusesforsurvival.com. www.diynaturalhomedeodorizers&airfreshners.com. I think that this would be a plus to businesses, even churches desiring <u>*favorable and/or healthier*</u> environments. Can we work together in some ways to help protect each other from negative spirit intentions?

There are other reasons like some foods that can also cause one to itch as a reaction or allergy, however some spirit energetic intrusion can deplete nutrition and/or proteins, causing the same reactions that some foods do and/or deplete nutrition that once was sufficient. Always check with your doctor, nutritionist and/or dermatologist, if not sure and/or see www.foodsthatcancause bodyitching.com. www.allergy/histamineintolerance.com

The Capital District Vitality Center, at 140 Lapp Rd, Clifton Pk., New York, 12065. Dr. Richard Herbold, Phone 518.371.6431, did a internet article on Histamine Intolerant.

**- Hand system functions:** They are predominantly controlled by the opposite brain hemisphere, so that the preferred hand choice reflects a brain functioning ability.

Excessive energy can cause stiffness, soreness, aches, discoordination, paralysis thereby affecting hand gestures, or any communicating with the hand(s), even one's ability to be helpful and caring. It indicates one's ability to work. Hands store water, fat and vitamin D. Energies on assignment will seem to constantly try to penetrate the hands/wrist or fingers, wherever they can to intrude upon the use of your hands and/or your service to the Lord. Wearing cloth and/or padded or cut-off gloves (leaving the fingers and thumb free) can be helpful. Also, if energy is showing up to be a nuisance while typing or whatever and you have on fitted gloves, you can take a small piece of paper towel and put witch hazel, vinegar or some peppermint extract on it and place it between the glove and your hand and you should find some release, some peace and the ability to continue what you were doing in Jesus name. **Also, it will protect your work from the excessive energy spirit being's ability to transfer onto your work.**

Spiritual Goal: **Keep hands free from excess or series of negative energy spirit intrusions and/ or penetrations in this area.** One can also place vinegar and water in a towel and continually dip whatever hand in the bowl to keep hands released from excess energy that has the ability to cause stiffness to various levels of hand paralysis. Actually, I have kept a vinegar and water bowl near my bed so, if I am awakened by excess spirit energy activity on my hand, I will awake to dip my hand in this substance. Put on gloves then go back to sleep. There was a tabloid showing hands of young people that had aged considerably; yep, it is caused by excess spirit energy activity nibbling on their hands (usually at night, but their potential is 24/7, revealing their energetic spirit *intention* is to harm that area, and/or to be able to process ones hands for their use, as the energetic beings will 2Tim 2.26, which could become serious).

Wear gloves and check to see if any beings affected in this area are losing certain nutrients levels. Also, you can set an alarm to awake you, just to make sure your limbs are protected and covered. This is also the type of energetic spirit activity that can and does happen in hotels. Some energies stay and often collect in the bathroom. Some energetic beings have the ability to put hotel visitors into a sleep state while the subject is relaxing in the tub and/or in bed. It would be safer if this is happening to you, you could use a vinegar and/or peppermint spray if needed to protect oneself from possible energetic spirit catastrophes during any bath time, as you pay attention, if while bathing you suddenly feel sleepy. You could also awake periodically throughout the night, just to wipe yourself off if you sense any excess energy activity that has disturbed the hands and/or one's body with any excess heat causing a dampness and/or numbness, or perhaps simply the ability to gestate any part of the body it found, consistently abiding. **Diet, exercise (like a hand ball) and prayer are important.**

It is also necessary to say that at places like license bureaus and/or doctor's offices where eyes are continually being checked on a eye machine are not being affected by people that are carrying excess energy upon their hands. As it will cause a abnormal and/or unusual distraction for those whose job depends on the accuracy of these machines to be free from excess energies that can affect normal eye vision. This is important. Hands that continually handle these machines should be washed before and after each person uses it. I was given an eye check and nothing was wiped off, and I did sense excess energies upon the machine. We may be able to save other people's jobs that depend on the accuracy of these machines. Thank you!

---

*Pictures at the end of this writing reveal some of the marks they can leave on the hand (like piercings when they want to get into the blood) and other parts of the body, and even parts of the inside of a vehicle reveals that some energetic spirit activity have the ability to manifest heat throughout a leather and cloth passenger car seat, and literally cause the seat covers to split causing it to look as if someone, perhaps an older child, could have used a sharp instrument to cut the seat. However, this was done by nuancing negative spirit energy activity, ritualistically over time, it would tear one row at a time until there were around 3 or 4 rows cut into the fabric.*

**- Feet system functions:** for movement and can effect one's ability to work. Enjoy life. Did you know that *most of the muscles that control the movement of your foot are located in your lower legs*?

Excess spirit energy activity: can affect things like ones circulatory system, muscles, and can cause stiffness, paralysis and even inflammation etc., the longer the energy engages you. *If there is no resistance to any energetic spirit activity or manifestations concerning the feet.* If you find your feet seemingly becoming numb you may need magnesium. It could also be an energetic method or means to get you to take your shoes off. Energetic spirit activity in ones shoe can also cause a person's foot to get stuck in their shoe. It seems that some level of excess energetic activity can cause these energetic beings to swell up in your shoe, causing it (your shoe) to become very tight until it either forces your foot out of your shoe, or causes your foot to become stuck in the shoe. Pouring vinegar into one's shoe can cause the energetic being to release the foot from the shoe!

For those who wear shoes to protect their feet at night, sometimes the energetic spirit beings just like to squeeze the feet to wake you at night; some are assigned just to come and keep you up all night, and I do mean all night, if they can. Excess spirit energy manifesting in the foot area can cause pain in the arch of your foot. Excessive spirit energy activity can cause nutrition and/or a vitamin deficiency, even from the feet area. Also, extra padding in one's shoe can be helpful to aid ward off any harm that any energetic spirit energy could do to the feet (by the excessive heat upon or within the shoe they are able to manifest). It could also help be the cause of dry feet, as some energy try to lodge in the toe area seemingly in an effort or method to keep up with their subjects, and/or it's a way to keep themselves close to nourishment, some try to do it inconspicuously, but ultimately the discomfort would get your attention. Some will cause irritation by keeping dampness in the toe area, which would eventually effect the whole foot. Sprinkling corn starch on a paper towel and then placing this wrap over your foot before inserting foot into shoe can help protect from the dampness the energy can cause.

There is also a certain level of intelligent energy operating among spirit beings with the ability to actually pierce the feet (while in the shoe), and then cause it to be affected (and heal slowly), by each continual excess spirit energy released in this area or they can expand their energy in the shoe to squeeze the area they pierced to make sure it is sore. Some will wear padding within the shoe to secure foot protection to keep the energy spirit activity from going into the body (through the feet area). Some will pierce the foot to keep you from wrapping it. I would wrap it any way and just get larger shoes. This is where it can get interesting; I have seen some use actual peanut butter, placed mostly under the toes, some at the bottom of the feet (whichever area brings the most comfort). The bottom of the foot and/or underneath the toe is the area energetic spirit beings seem to try to draw out the nutrients. I also think the peanut butter can pacify them, and is the reason they dry it out; they are taking the nutrients out of it. The peanut butter can also help prevent the energies ability to move freely within your shoe, causing discomfort when you walk. Then, the foot with the peanut butter can be placed on layered paper towels, wrapped on the foot (to the subjects comfort, and may need to be adjusted as the alien spirit energies are able to seemingly heat). Energies can dry out the inside of the shoe in order to melt or dry out the peanut butter to get to the foot (if you can wrap your head around this), while the subject is resting and/or sleeping. This is what they are able to do. I also believe that the peanut butter and foot wrap will aid in protecting one's feet from energetic spirit beings ability to web the feet. I have even heard of a person having a cleft foot (where there are no toes). www.pictureofalienwebfeet.com. Also see: www.babywebfeet.com.

Whenever the energy penetrates the foot wrap (if it causes you to wake and/or becomes discomforting), simply put on another application of peanut butter wrapped in a paper towel within the shoe upon waking. For those who desire to sleep with their shoes on, should double tie it, as some level of alien spirit energies are able to untie shoe strings and even pull at the shoe and/or shoe string until the shoe is loose enough to push off and/or cause the subject to push the shoe off by numbing the foot in the shoe. Actually, when they try to numb the feet while you are sleeping it is to try to get you to subconsciously feel the discomforts so you will end up kicking your own shoe(s) off. Also, magnesium can help offset the numbness. So, coming into the body through the feet area must be important to them (their comfort at your expense). Remember, all they can bring to the table is (Jn. 10.10) their spirit DNA, no matter how energetic beings are able to deceive many, Rev. 16.10. It is hard to imagine that some people call these beings nice or benevolent. If so, this tells me that they can be who they need to be to get their job done. Some people can be deceived by kindness. Again, revealing the need to teach more effectively on other worldly beings, not just the good side.

They (the alien spirit beings) not only want control of certain areas of their subject (or people's lives), but they want absolute freedom to come and go as they please, within and/or concerning the subjects body, which is really unsettling, seeing that they have the potential to want to also connect strange relationships for their purpose and control, or cause division among the cultures, family, politics and even communities. *It seems to be how these beings DNA are "wired"!* Those they have processed seemingly through the night *are those the beings are more able to seize their bodies during the day causing a type of energetic forced servitude*, in community and use them to cause whatever trouble or communications they are desiring. It is something to watch play out once you learn their spirit DNA activity! These are fallen energetic spirit beings (reinventing themselves as alien spirit space brothers as some call them) seemingly trying to resurrect their lives in our nation and among us. These are some of the energetic methods used to cause harm in the lives and families of those who need to learn how to recognize and resist alien spirit intentions and activity, just to keep the family together. Ja. 4.7. These *are just my suggestions* that helped me to keep free to do what the Lord was requiring. So I had to resist, like all of us who desire to serve the Lord, which they try hard to stop. I pray this writing reaches the many in need, in Jesus name!

These beings really don't want you to know, nor realize, that there are only two spiritual kingdom activities going on among us, *only two*. They want everyone to stay confused over the "religion"/ "religious or non-religious" issues. So everyone needs to realize which spiritual energetic kingdom they are operating in intentionally and/or being forced to operate in and learn how to recognize and release (or resist) dark, prophetic, negative energetic spirit activity (moving prophetically among us), especially those in positions among us (and the spirit beings operating through them want acknowledgment) because these negative spirit energies love to reveal themselves through people in positions, so all the other energies operating among us can see who they were able to overcome, or who needs to learn how to resist them still. But the most important trait that these spirit beings seem to reflect through others that don't resist them is their "dumbness." It seems to be their (energetic beings) trademark. I am not calling anyone dumb. Paul said they were dumb. So dumb is what dumb does. Corin. 12.2. Reflecting that a certain level of release and/or healing is needed of those who these beings have managed to affect. How dumb is it to keep families arguing, divided, and cultures always having unresolved issues when we all need the same things. Not to mention the sexual confusion they create *just because they can find a place to operate*. Spirits don't have a gender, it's the confusion and disharmony they feed off of. JESUS, please, our land is in need of understanding of spirit beings operating energetically among us! Jn. 10.10. Corin. 12.2.

**Spiritual Goal:** To preserve the feet, try to keep them padded and protected from negative energetic beings targeting the feet area. There is a need to gain the ability to **slow** down if not stop the process of the alien spirit being intentions regarding you. **Diet and prayer are important.** Also, the flowcharts that we use are able to help people resist any potential seizes in the community, **to help keep one from being used to further alien agenda. How? The words of Jesus are also considered energy and Jesus is the word. *So we need to focus during any energetic activity, by resisting it, until it lifts*. So any festering and or rising energetic spiritual conflicts can be quenched, in Jesus name. He did promise in His word to be a shield.** Ps.18.30. **A safe place. This is important when other worldly spirit beings are here intentionally trying to work through men's flesh** (body, soul and spirit), **not sometimes, but continually! It is their DNA** (energetic spirit beings are driven). **It's how they roll! This is serious!**

*The name of the Lord is a strong tower, the righteous runneth into it and is safe.*
*Proverbs 18.10.*

## - Skeletal (bone) system functions: as the body's framework; which includes bones, connective tissue and internal organs.

Excessive energy can effect any part of your bone structure. 2Ki.13.21. Especially if negative spiritual energy is able to gestate upon your body at night with little or no resistance, nor interruption. Here it is able to deeply penetrate itself into the bones and cause them to become weak or brittle, causing a weak frame and brittle bones where affected. Weak bones are able to put a strain on other parts of the body.

**Spiritual Goal:** <u>Realize</u> when certain negative spirit energies seem to come (ritually and/or consistently) upon the body in certain areas causing discomfort and/or heat, especially at night. If so, test it by placing vinegar and water (and/or peppermint and water) on a towel and place over the affected area (or an area being energetically distressed). The vinegar has to be strong enough, if the discomfort and/or heat releases, great. You should get some kind of a response. <u>www.thevinegaranniversarybookbyemilythacker.com</u>.

Potentially, excessive spirit energy gestating consistently upon any part of the body (regularly can potentially cause functional and/or developmental disorders, by initially weakening the area).This can be done at night when the excess spirit energies can and will manifest under the body as one sleeps if there is no resistance. Energy spirits on assignment are intelligent beings and are also able to potentially cause accidents in home or wherever, making it easier for them to attach to the body when it is still then they can gestate, into even deeper gestations to affect and/or disrupt the bone system. I wonder if many doctors might realize the potential of these beings, often it is only revealed to those they are assigned to (or those being affected by spirit energetic beings). See DVD, <u>www.unawaredvd.com</u> .

For example, Paget's disease can affect the pelvis, spine, legs or skull. All are areas where energies can be found manifesting consistently. We must be taught, with understanding, how to discern harmful, energetic spirit beings and then learn how to remedy these experiences.

Another example is of patients with skeletal fluorosis, who show side effects from high fluoride doses that can come from ruptures in the stomach lining. Fluorine can also damage the parathyroid glands leading to hyperparathyroidism, which is the uncontrolled secretion of parathyroid hormones (part of endocrine system).These hormones regulate calcium concentration in the body. So let's go back for a moment. <u>What can be a potential cause for rupture in the stomach lining. Excessive energy consistently manifesting and/or being released in this area can potentially cause this, also depending on how each person is effected by excess energy</u>. And an elevated parathyroid hormone concentration in the body can cause a calcium deficiency in bone structures and a higher calcium concentrate in the blood. As a result bone flexibility decreases. I believe a lot of diseases can be prevented if we learn to know when we are dealing with other worldly spirit energies that spiritually or energetically engage us. I understand that issues with heredity and physical impairment can weigh in, but there is excessive spirit energy that can also come into play, should we throw the possible baby out with the bathwater? Corin. 14.30-32. Dt. 29.29. <u>www.skeletalfluorosis</u>. I guess the point I am trying to make is that excessive spirit energy activity upon the body can affect healthy nutrition and vitamin levels. A timer, set at intervals, or alarm clock, could also prove helpful to check if your clothes are still dry, and/or a change of clothes is needed. **Diet and prayer are important!**

## - Muscular system functions; Includes all muscles in the body, movement of voluntary
muscles, movement of organs (involuntary muscles); they maintain body temperature and posture. <u>www.musclefunction.com.</u>

Excessive spirit energy activity gestating consistently and/or ritually upon the body can also seem to potentially weaken and/or deteriorate the muscular system. Babies and young children, as well as adults, can also be affected by too much excess energy. Mk 9.21.

There are many different types of muscle diseases that can also potentially be caused by excess negative spirit energy operating and/or gestating within and/or upon the body. As an example, predominant symptoms for _Pompe Disorder_ would include some of the following:

> One of the first signs can be delayed motor ability(s); with walking, then with climbing stairs, gait abnormalities
>
> Progressive muscle weakness (beginning with the trunk and proximal muscles, then lower limbs)
>
> Limb girdle muscle weakness, muscle pain, frequent falls
>
> Respiratory involvement could also result from degeneration of diaphragm, and other respiratory muscles may manifest as respiration insufficiency … Indications of sleep disorders
>
> Daytime fatigue www.pompedisorder.com

What I find interesting is that potentially, in this writing, I have indicated that many of these areas, just listed, can also be affected by excess spirit energy activity, which is likely to manifest, rest or gestate in the limb trunk of the body. This article goes on to say that general outcomes vary for different people. And that is also true if, for example, you have excess energy working on same family members and/or friends, since everyone's intake level of energetic spirit tolerance is different, there would be different outcomes or symptoms for each. This article goes on to say that some patients may experience relatively mild symptoms for years, followed by an abrupt clinical decline, which can occur at any time. This is exactly their (spirit energetic activity's) method; to energetically spirit penetrate their subject continually (on a daily basis) in a progressive manner. Day by day (so far I have had to deal with many of the above symptoms and sometimes it seems that more advanced energy spirit beings will try to hurry up the physical degeneration process, and then give back the daily degenerative practices to the lesser spirit energetic activities). This is a dark spirited kingdom activity in operation today.

I think the only thing that has guarded and protected me from this type, or any type, of muscle degeneration is my relationship with the Lord, who literally taught me how to discern negative spirit energy activity by the symptoms that these beings were trying to manifest in different parts of the body. 2Tim 1.12.  How the Lord seemingly was able to walk me safely through each degenerative process, or other negative intentions of negative energetic spirit activity of darkness, as they arose, according to the contents of this writing. Such as awakening me when my clothes needed changing, due to heat that alien spirit beings are able to create. And when they have tried to press in (meaning turn up the heat) is when I would not hesitate to fling bottles of vinegar, circling around me to discourage my enemy. Because God said, no weapon formed against me shall prosper in Jesus name. However, these beings must be resisted, in Jesus name. James 4.7. Isa. 54.17. Biblically, we are told to be courageous, and the Lord will be with the good. Dt. 31.6. Ps. 27.14. And since negative energy tries to take up our space (my space, or your space) when they come and/or when they get ridiculous I fill my space with vinegar, which is a radical element. We must learn to engage that which engages us on whatever level it reveals itself.

> The kingdom of heaven suffers violence …
> and the violent take it by force.
>
> Mt. 11.12.

And when the energy lifts, I give God praise, in Jesus name. For this is the day that the Lord has made, I will rejoice and be glad in it. Amen! Then, I tell my kids, to preserve their lives in the earth, for the secret things revealed are for us and our children. Amen. Thank you Lord. Amos 3.7. Dan. 2.21-22.

**Spiritual Goal:** If energy seems to operate around the subject usually at night, usually during sleep times, and the subject awakes feeling uncomfortable and perhaps damp consistently, one must pay close attention to all body symptoms, and perhaps journalize the symptoms and conditions of the body upon waking. If need be, begin to set your alarm to wake up to check on yourself periodically throughout the night and, if need be, change into whatever area of the body is in need of dryer clothes. **Also diet, prayer, and alarm clock and/or timer could be helpful.**

## - Red and White blood cell system. 
The colorless cells of the immune system circulate in the blood and lymph. The white blood cell count is made in the bone marrow, so _radiation_ (or certain levels of heat upon the body) to the bone can suppress the blood cell count. The body needs amino acids from protein to make new WBC and vitamin B-12 is helpful and good. Cleanliness is important and relevant during low WBC (white blood count).

Excessive spirit energy activity that is able to gestate and permeate upon the body and into the blood stream can cause nutritional and vitamin deficiency. **Spiritual Goal:** Realize when spirit energy is trying to consistently affect you, and find a way to resist and/or release yourself from it (naturally and energetically, or spiritually so). **Diet and prayer are important.** Also, it is good to wipe oneself off first thing in the morning from any possible, yet unrealized excess spirit energy activity operating upon and/or within the body daily.

- **Weight function:** Fitness should be a function of body weight. Excessive spirit energy activity can and will not only add excess energy (coming through as heat to create excess body fat) to your normal body weight, but also has the ability to seemingly create space within the body and literally expand itself (within your body while you sleep seems to be a preferred time, and they come with confidence because seemingly no one knows, or really realizes, you need to deal with them on this level, because who can even get this far in the discussion, perhaps only those with experience). James 4.7. Some energetic spirit beings just don't care. They just bull-doze into the body anyway, potentially causing burning sensations upon entry of certain lower private body parts, including the hands in order to make room for itself to enter and exist in the body, and then nourishes itself in the body, as if they made hotel reservations in advance. This, in fact, to the natural eye looks like weight gain or puffy look on the hands, but_does not_ necessarily come from extra eating! I woke one day wondering why no one told me I was gaining weight, as I don't get a chance to look in a full length mirror often. And when I did, I said where did all _this come from, as I had not remembered stuffing myself for any particular reason, but was more conscious to fast, because I really needed the Lord's help and protection to sort through all this extra-curricular demonic alien spirit energetic being activity happening among us._

## Getting your rest

Alternate ways to deal with excess spirit energy activity in the mornings (or through the night), when you sense spirit energy activity trying to get or trying to affect the body, and use your faith to deal with them, using the flowchart, around 20-30 min. (for one side of the chart, twice the time for both sides) and this could potentially help you fall back to sleep. This could play out for 15 plus years of resisting their intentions. Ask the lady bowed down in the church for 18 years. Lk. 13.11. Ps. 38.6. Still, we need to get rest for the body's sake. For some, Melatonin, by vitafusion in tablets, liquid or gummies is a natural ingredient to help get to sleep. Others may need the doctor to recommend something stronger.

Any energetic activity operating in the above areas can also do what we may call, "bum rush you", meaning, if they are really trying to press in to any particular system of the body, they are able to seemingly affect two or more of any of the above categories at once! Causing you to think some-thing serious could be wrong with you. But we all need to learn how to deal with excess spirit energy activity coming from seemingly other worldly realms, as soon as it engages you, breaking through time and space into a human realm. They can't seem to function on a certain human level, without attaching to another life form in our realm. One of their goals seems to be to keep us so distracted with ill physical symptoms and energetic episodes (of busyness), and in this way keep us from focusing on the things of God and forgetting that we sit in heavenly places in Christ Jesus, and that we need to pray from this perspective. Eph. 2.6.

Perhaps this is one of the reasons the Barna Group Research studies reflect an estimated 70% of people in the NE are not reading their bible. www.stateofabible2015report-americanbiblesociety.com. One way for us to not feed into these statistics (and/or not become a statistic) is by off-setting the negative spirit energetic distractions by keeping a vinegar spray bottle (mixed with water and peppermint, or whichever you choose to your liking) nearby, so that when the distractions come while you are trying to read your bible, and/or meditate upon the Lord, just spray around yourself until the distractions stop (or during any energetic distractions), then you will know that there are energies trying to operate in your environment (as a energetic spiritual kingdom opposition). We need to biblically and spiritually recognize the only two spiritual kingdom operations happening among us. One is constantly distracting you from the things of God. So now we know what we need to do in this situation. Praise the Lord! Mt. 7.15-20.

Any of the categories above potentially can be many of the causes of some of today's statistical concerns and even creations for sickness, disease and mental concerns. There seems to be a marvelous ministry service available in any church for a nutritionist, especially during this rise and seemingly deep energetic activity happening among us!

# Mind functions to think, feel and want, according to www.westsidetoastmasters.com

Excessive spirit energy targets the head (effects not only the head, but potentially the mind). They say a mind is a terrible thing to waste. And, I think, a mind is a terrible thing for someone to take!

*Are we dealing with the symptoms or the energy? Or should we be dealing with the symptoms, or the energy causing the symptoms? Are we dealing with the symptoms because of the energy, or do we deal with the energy to prevent the symptoms?*

---

Radiant energy is a form of kinetic energy. Kinetic energy refers to the movement of the energy whether it is of atoms, molecules, waves, substance or objects. Radiant energy is the result of a change in configuration of electrons. It can travel through any substance, including air, liquid, glass and space. Even in a vacuum environment, radiant energy can move. And it is the energetic spirit beings penetrating spirit energy activity upon the body that makes it radiate. OK. So, now we need to learn how to detect their movement upon the body. Because they always come upon the body for a purpose!

Does it sound like energy can recreate itself, in its own likeness? Genesis 1.

Radiant energy moves in a straight line at a very high speed and can be absorbed, transmitted or reflected … If the energy is only partially able to penetrate the object, then it is absorbed. The energy is not transmitted if an object cannot absorb it. www.radiantenergy.com

chapter 3

# Community

Communities seemingly are being energetically effected by segments of society, in the manner of a procession. Many are being synergistically effected by energetic beings to accomplish their intentions among us, seemingly to cause confusion, disorder or disarray among us, keeping us in a surface only reality (even a type of ill-prophetic activity and operation causing people to take at face value what they see in the natural, as evidence to judge what's going on, or by who is causing it) **by what one is seeing only**; bible reveals this can be a spiritual blindness-John 9.39. Rom 11.8. Isa 43.8. Rom 8.7-8. Eph 2.2.Gal.3.1. 2Corin. 4:3-4, that is by:

> Sectioning, subdivision, etc., literally causing us to fragment ourselves, by way of energetically affecting, or afflicting segments or sections of our society. I wonder would these types of ongoing negative effects on humanity cause another void? Gen 1.2.

It is not my intention to purposely offend anyone, especially the gods, even if that's seemingly not hard to do. They seem to always be at best a bundle of nerves, and this result is reflective in those they energetically effect, it seems to make-up their DNA personality, and the bible reveals and teaches you, know them by their fruit (some can see the spiritual fruit, some can only see the natural fruit but don't know how to judge it, evidenced by what is seemingly being allowed among us). Really! Mt. 12. Nevertheless, there is a need to get through this teaching and explanation of how and why our society is being influenced as it is. It is really sad that our alien beings have been energetically effecting us for around 50 years now and it seems that this energetic spirit activity (of darkness and disaster) is closer to home, that everyone is actually paying more attention to the ill-will, physical harm and/or sin of these alien beings are creating in our lives and in the lives of those around us.

As we stated in our introduction, that the people in Acts 14 said, "the gods have come down to us in the likeness of men." How is that possible? That the gods are able to transform themselves … into the likeness of men! Well, we can look biblically at Judas and say, "wasn't he affected by the gods or a god," other than the most High God, even though he seemed to operate among the apostles (or the godly). We know Judas was different by the spirit or energetic fruit activity that seemingly caused him to turn on Jesus.

But Jesus said unto him, "Judas, betrayest thou the Son of man with a kiss?" Lk. 22.28.

Therefore, betrayal also seems to fit the DNA fruit of the gods that come down and/or effect those likewise (into their image) is how they influence those among us. Like the God who affects or causes his people to pray among us with those who prey. Lk 612. The work of the flesh is the work(s) or DNA of the gods', Gal 5. It is the flesh (and/or gods operating in one's soul acting out through the flesh body), producing flesh activity, energetically manifesting through the souls of men. And what Paul said in Galatians seems to apply to our generation as we are literally observing the "gods" acting out "flesh" (or activating out as flesh behavior) through the souls of men. Gal. 5.

Upon study and the process of time it seems that demons can gain the ability to reinvent themselves (in the souls they gain by energetic means) then continue to hide as alien beings. www.forbiddenknowledge.com. Some call them aliens, some call themselves alien brothers. These aliens have learned by engaging with our armies and scientists, in their own methods of mind communication and (through the personality DNA of deception) were able to experiment at first, with our animals and then, with our humanity. These energetic beings found out that we were compatible for their breeding purposes, according to the readings in the book reference and available internet sources. Please excuse me, but I feel like I am trying to write to cause others to be aware in an effort to help others protect themselves, while still trying to get over the shock, that this spiritual (alien) energetic activity *is really happening to us!*

Now, that we can understand that our alien, now seemingly self-energetically forced (itself into our world) resident beings, did not stop experimenting with our armies and scientists as it initially intended *(or were they just too effected by the beings to resist their hidden intentions that are effecting us now)*, but now we need to understand why and how they are energetically effecting our society, one person at a time *(like leaven hidden in meal)*, even as they have seemingly effected our armies and scientists. You may ask, what makes me think and/or say that our armies and scientists were effected by the alien beings.

> BECAUSE EVIDENTLY THEY DID NOT AND/OR COULD NOT STOP HOW THE ALIENS HAVE CONTINUED TO INTRUDE INTO OUR SOCIETY. WHAT THEY ARE DOING AMONG US AS WE CONTINUE TO WATCH THEM CAPTIVATE AND CAPTURE OUR SOCIETY, CAUSING SOME OF US MENTAL ANGUISH, SOCIAL ILLS AND OTHER PHYSICAL IMPAIRMENT AND/OR PRE-MATURE DEATH.

> WHOEVER REMAINS, THESE BEINGS SEEM TO USE US AS A SOURCE OF NOURISHMENT, AS WELL AS AVENUES TO AVANCE THEIR ALIEN AGENDA AMONG US.

Similarly, many of us are found to be the object of alien affection (biblically viewed as gods or snare disguised). Dt 7.17. As they are obviously acting out in the lives of those who could not, or did not, realize how to resist their intentions – after all who is teaching it?

In this writing, I have tried to reveal ways and energetic methods of how alien beings can potentially and energetically effect our bodies (behind closed doors, with daily ritualistic intruding visitations) and in time, some are entangled in dark ill-spirited service, weakened, disabling others to make it easier to take over their bodies, souls and eventually the lives of others by these slow daily ritualistic visitations, making their death appear like a natural process, but actually induced by negative energetic ritualistic intruding visitations, and potentially sometimes they want our minds to not work. However, what is interesting about the mind is that the aliens may use one or two processes to gain entrance:

> People that do <u>not yet</u> realize that guarding their minds with the name of Jesus can potentially protect them from losing their mind from energetic bombarding thoughts of nonsense that these beings can create and/or cause.

> Many need to realize and understand that the words of Christ are energy, positive, healing energy, and energy is power. Power that we can use to resist any negative thought patterns (as battling a type of mind bombardment).

> We use an anatomy chart along with our faith chart of the names and acts of Jesus, by which to resist negative energies that come against the mind and/or different parts of the body.

The issue is that our nation, every segment of our nation, is being effected by dark spirited energetic intentions. As we move from season to season as a family, city, community and nation, you can literally tell how the energetic beings are moving through these areas of our lives by the civil crimes and/or attacks manifesting through our news. When people are being attacked, it is because the person attacking is usually being effected, and directed in their attacking initiatives literally by alien agenda. You know them by their fruit is not just a slogan. Mt. 12. It can literally point us to who is needing to learn how to resist dark spirited energetic intentions and initiatives.

The concern is, and should be, that we gain a spiritual/biblical knowledge of handling ourselves when arising spiritual energetic concerns happen among us as a nation, state, city, local community or world community; we are as strong as our weakest part.

Therefore, needing to deal with energies trying to effect us **is not the same** as spiritual or states of mental conditions of those who may not mind being diagnosed, because they really do need help. So why is there confusion with some in these professions that have a need to mistakenly force some who visit a hospital for very different health concerns, being seemingly coerced into taking medication for a coined mental condition one may not have, or who may have a better understanding of energetic spirit activity, but just got caught up in one of their plots?

Correspondingly, we may also need to deal with growing symptoms of professionals and/or leaders who also are being spiritually effected, perhaps at a faster rate than the clients needing their help. This makes sense if you consider that it is an energetic strategy among us for these beings to energetically process those in positions of interest to these beings where they can effect the most people. The concern is that many effected can no longer perceive that they have been energetically spiritually affected to endorse affected alienist views. A good example is listening to the news on September 19, 2015 around 10-11am hour on the 103.3 FM radio dial, where I heard President Obama's concern for taking a closer look at our Justice system, because the president said:

"There is something wrong when this many people are being locked up."

Then, I thought, due to alien infiltration in many souls it would be a good idea to revisit all systems that make up our society because the aliens are, and have been, energetically effecting all systems that make up our society and are refocusing them to "fit" alien agendas.

Accounting for the reality of what happens when medications begin to fail at a faster and faster rate, due to the reality that beings are able to operate around different meds to accomplish their energetic intrusion in their subject's life. This scenario could apply to all professions, not only those who some view to be in psychotic states of being.

Perhaps it is a good time to ask, what does a society energetically effected by alien beings pressing forward to take over look like? 2Tim 2.26.

> Genesis 6, says there were giants on the earth in those days … Then the Lord saw that the wickedness of men was great in the earth and that every intent of the thought of man's heart was only evil continually.
>
> V. 6; Here the Lord's answer to this experience seems to be to destroy the earth.
>
> So we can see that negative energetic beings can and do have a negative effect on man and society

Please pray with me, Lord please, we repent, help us to recover and restore our humane caring society, uncontrolled and undominated by other worldly beings. Lk 18.1. Rev. 2.5. Rev. 2.21. Rev. 9.21. Rev. 2.16.

## chapter 4

# Segments of our Society are Changing Directly Due to Ongoing Energetic Activity Operating Among Us

*No, they are not all benevolent!*

We want to look at how energetic beings are effecting our systems of society. Whether TV or radio, I am always listening for voices of people that seem to have an understanding of what is happening among us, even though they may not know why. I listened as a guy called into a radio talk show, 103.3FM, around August or September, 2015. A guy began to tell the talk show host that there seemed to be a deep work of darkness happening among us. And I thought, that is exactly right, a dark spiritual hostile kingdom take over is a process to pull a society into a deep, deep place and work the operation of darkness among us.

We seem as a nation to better see the effects of sin on other nations, than ourselves, but we seem to get stumped when we not only walk in sin, effected by it, not to mention the effects of being literally sucked more and more into sin by the hidden, yet obvious works of energetic beings. It is what they do! Satan and his angels were kicked out of heaven … there is nothing new under the sun. We just need to learn *how* *to* resist the enemies intentions for our nation one individual at a time … an energetic hidden activity that has been unfolding and recorded initially by psychologists via a process of hypnosis, and is now coming out of the hidden into our realities. Realities of those especially who have been able to survive their hostile excessive, energetic abuses though excessive spiritual activity. It is a biblical truth, as well as a present reality, that energetic spirit activity can effect the physical body as well as the soul. Lk. 3.35. Lk 9.39. Rev. 12.7-12. James 4.7.

# Suicide

Suicide was once considered more of a moral issue; now it is considered more of a medical concern. Jennifer Michael Hecht, author of A History of Suicide and the Philosophies Against It said suicide is wrong. She said that suicide harms the community and that it also damages yourself in the future.
www.thecastastropheofsuicide-catholicededucationsourcecenter.com

The Society for the Prevention of Teen Suicide reveals how real the problem is:

> - Suicide is the 3rd leading cause of teen death
>
> - For every suicide completion, there are 50-200 attempts
>
> - The suicide attempt rate among teens is increasing ages 10-14

www.techervision/teensuicide.com

Updates for Mental Health Professionals regarding children and trauma, by the American Psychological Association and the Presidential Task Force on Post Traumatic Stress Disorder and Trauma in Children and Adolescents in 2008:

States that a traumatic event is one that threatens injury, death or physical integrity of self or others, and can also cause horror, terror and/or helplessness at the time it occurs. Includes sexual abuse, physical abuse, domestic violence, community and school violence, medical trauma, motor vehicle accidents, acts of terrorism, natural and human made disasters, suicides and other traumatic losses. Surely, this should include hostile spiritual energetic intrusion from other worldly beings that have the ability to create and/or cause any of these symptoms ...

Suicide can cause generational deformities; physical, mental and emotional deficiencies, as well as victimization and/or family violence. Community and society are also a potential due to energetic agendas and realities operating among us.

Some countries are still using 17th century tactics to "protect society"; abandoning and confining the mad in asylums or psychiatric facilities, often for life, which helps to compound the negative impact of mental issues on individuals and society as a whole. www.worldbank.org (The zero hour for mental health). M.facebook.com, www.modernhealthcare.com www.blog.massmed.org; www.scriptureagainstsuicide, hopefaithprayer.com

Growing Police stories

Mental health within law enforcement is noticing that police suicide follows violent crimes. A new mental health strategy among the police community in this article stated that 38% of long term sick leave among regular police and civilian members were caused by mental issues. www.cbc.ca

Police stories that went south spiraling into catastrophes:

CBS news; www.cbc.ca – Troubled cops need help

www.killedbypolicel.net

www.policeshootingofinnocentcivilians

www.clevelandcarchaseendswithtwodead137shotsfired

www.investigationoftheclevelanddivisionofpolice

www.mousouripolicediscriminathighwaydrivers.com

## Hospital and/or Doctors care:

Most published research is found to be false … refuted by other subsequent evidence. The claim of false research findings can be proven. This article examines facts that can cause or feed into false research. www.falsedpublihedresearch.com

There are doctors giving unnecessary health care treatment for a profit. Some people, processed by energetic beings become vessels for their intentions. www.people/july/2015.com.

One writer speaks on the mass poisoning of humanity; an exploration of human stupidity, on how human beings are the only species stupid enough to actually poison themselves. That we create a wide range of chemical toxins that go into the ecosystem through rivers and streams, the soul, air, etc … and then we synthesize toxic chemicals and put them directly into our food supply. Knowing that they can be poisonous and contribute to the epidemic rates of ongoing diseases we are facing today. www.naturalnews.com/008511. We are what we eat, www.wearewhatweeat-thepoisoningofourfoodsupply/farmwars.com

There are articles insinuating that mysterious doctors' deaths in various states were being targeted and killed in a wide-ranging conspiracy. Some have disappeared without a trace. Again, we need to point out that we, individually and as a society, are not recognizing the potential harm that can be done by ill-energetic activity working independently and/or through others these beings have effected. Let's just say what happens if our doctors do not take seriously the potential of ill-energetic activity operating among us. If our doctors are being removed by that which they are not understanding and recognizing, then what will the people do? www.aremedicinesfinetbe-ingassassinated.com. This is another reason for this writing, to teach people how to recognize the harm of on-going negative energetic activity operating in anyone's life; to help preserve life, family, community and humanity. www.allnewspipeline.com .

There are many that go to emergency, looking for a simple remedy, only to find themselves being held because a doctor is declaring them with mental concerns, when the actual issue is more nutritional, or a questionable judgment call by the doctor due to a nutritional situation, never checked out, nor considered, causing one to ask why? Are alien beings causing men to be inhumane towards man? Can we perceive there is another agenda operating among us?

# Education

Educational concerns include the suicides among its youth across the nation.

The New York City school chancellor, Carmen Farina, held a private meeting with principals to discuss the suicide epidemic among city students. This topic was also addressed first by the New York Post. Stating that suicides are rising among its city's youth.

In March, 2014, 12 youth had committed suicide in New York. Also in March, 2014, volunteers gathered with 1,892 American flags in Washington at their National Mall, averaging 22 veteran suicides a day! Since 2001, about the time the Lord would begin the experiences that would give rise to this book, the Iraq and Afghanistan and other active duty soldiers found that more died from killing themselves than combat!

Universities as well are meeting growing demands and challenges for comprehensive mental health care. Suicide is the second leading cause of death among college-aged students. Dr. Sharma, a Director of Ohio State's counseling service, states that there are more students enrolled currently in higher education that have already been previously treated for a mental health problem than any other time in history. www.collegeusatoday.com

We understand the importance of preventative medicine. It is great to be able to share and maybe even network with others regarding the stress coming against the mind. However, talking may only delay the symptoms, but not necessarily prevent the symptoms and/or ongoing condition.

To deal with any ailment or mental symptom it needs to be put into a proper or better context. Because what people are being given are pills to help remove and/or deal with the symptoms, which is good, but we also need to realize that any pills given for stress can wear off. However, there are different types and levels of stress. Some people are just seemingly prone to be stressed often. Some people are motivated by the stress, realizing that once I get this home work done or test completed, my stress level will go back possibly to zero.

We also can realize that stress alone does not lead to suicide itself, it is the energy causing the stress (as symptoms of a by-product) is what people need to realize how to deal with. There is a type of energetic stress (that people need to learn how to recognize) that energetic beings can cause when they are either trying to attach to a life and/or person's life. We as a whole need to learn how to deal with what is engaging our society in light of this writing and the people need space and/or time in the workplace and/or school etc., to be excused without the drama (or the pressure of if their meds will wear off, which can help to produce sudden drama unexpectedly, anywhere, at anytime) just to deal with energy intrusions. These are the other cards on the table Americans need to deal with, an issue even bigger than "mental illness" because it is the negative energetic beings causing it!

## Policing & Security of local Businesses:

Rest areas, state parks and local businesses seem to be on an approximately 15 minute type of security interval that are seemingly being enforced by business and police in sync in agreement and police are found notified, usually it seems when it gets close to 15 minutes when certain patrons come on the scene.

You could also watch this particular system that seems to also be visually enforced (by surveillance video cameras) whenever certain cultures come on the scene and that has also been noted in the news and should be explored. Just suppose there was a race problem (although I believe the issue is a bit deeper than the seemingly surface race issues happening among us) however, it is said that most race incidents go unreported. We have witnessed:

- lighter cultures in business environments literally call security on a regular basis, whenever a darker cultured person comes on the scene, almost giving the impression that they use this system within business communities to keep track of darker cultures and if you wait long enough, within 15 min., police and/or security shows up. This behavior is not just limited to Ohio, but can appear that Ohio seems to be a more concentrated and/ or present area of this type of questionable behavior. Pavlov's theory still seems to work whether training a dog or a person by seemingly rewarding them for certain behavior. You begin to believe that a certain type of behavior is expected. I call monkey do behavior, because it (the behavioral activity is energetically inspired or sometimes expressed by a seige). So then where is the accountability to questionable behaviors seemingly being taught in community.

-We have seen police show up at a local shopping mall strip, and only seem to drive in front of darker patrons, a few lanes in front of a darker patron as this patron started their vehicle to leave, and while situating certain things in their vehicle another policeman pulls up between the darker patroned driver and the first policeman that came on the scene and just squared-off the darker patron driver (in a spooky manner). The darker patron notes the two policemen's positions, then drives past the policeman, goes to the nearest gas station and calls the police dept., in the Rt. 91 and I-90 highway area in Ohio. When the answering machine answered, the patron asked for someone in charge, then left a message that with all of the negative gung-ho police activity regarding police incidences being aired on TV and radio regarding darker cultures, why were these two policemen squaring off their vehicles with seemingly only darker cultures that come out of the (T) store in this area.***There was no return call***! I noticed surveillance cameras at this shopping strip mall.  So why would the police come on the scene when they notice black patrons in the monitored area?

- Then, I heard a news story on the radio where a light colored policeman was found wrestling with a black lady at a party, and those around the scene spoke up and said that it was not a crime to be black! Whoa, I thought. www.mobilenytimes.com www.mhuffpost.com.

Locally, we have seen a darker cultured person go to a local park to go for a walk for exercise and with in 15 minutes a policeman comes on the scene and parks near by this walker's car. OK, well, no big deal you think. However, when this person, who happens to be of a darker culture, leaves the park area and goes a few blocks over to a local store to buy shoes, this policeman mysteriously shows up and parks only a couple lanes over from their vehicle. Is this normal policing, to follow local patrons around causing them to feel unsafe, to say the least. Who should they call for protection, "the police"! Which one? Hopefully, the ones not displaying this unsettling behavioral issue! Now-a-days it seems like it is necessary to first deal with the police (seen) issues even before, you can deal with your own (which can be an issue the police are trying to give you, when they are not dealing with their _own energy_). Who are we to call for protection, when police are displaying their own overt personality issues! What type of policing is this? This was in the W. 117th area and Lorain, by W. 150th St., in Cleveland, Oh.

Then there is the incident, where one of our workers travelled to a local Walmart, at exit 169 off I-71 South of Cleveland, when they got there parked, and noticed that someone, a lady, suddenly pulled almost in front of our worker and then began to stare at our worker, as our worker wondered why, our worker decided to move because they felt uncomfortable to get out of the car by someone behaving strange.

As our driver pulled the car closer to the Walmart store, our driver noticed that suddenly someone else pulled up in front of her and got out of the car, and began to look around their vehicle. Ok, our driver thought.

Our driver wondered why these 2 vehicles would pull up at the same time (in sync) as our driver drove in to park at this Walmart. As our driver got out of the car and began walking towards the Walmart entrance doors, suddenly there is a guy coming on the scene walking quickly towards a path, soon to cross the path of our worker; as they were both walking towards Walmart, our driver noticed this particular man about to cross her path headed towards the Walmart store. This man was on the phone, that spoke quickly in a volume she could hear, as she felt these 3 people seemingly over concerned with her, even though she did not know any of these people.

Suddenly, the person closest to Walmart spoke on the phone to someone while observing our worker out of the corner of their eye saying, "when I tell you … come running!" Dear Lord, I thought who are they talking about as our driver looked around, she _seemed to be the only one_ in the parking lot when this occurred. Our driver wondered if these were undercover cops due to their behavior. Were they having some type of imaginative delusion, our worker thought? Was anyone of them on meds? Did the meds wear off? Is this what happens when officers are at any shopping community … shouldn't our officer be trained regarding how to realize when what they are watching becomes fantasy and when they are watching actual reality in process? Or will we, as a community, take for granted our officers are self-sufficient, that they can tell when they need help? Well, when would this happen? How many civilians do our officers have to pull into their fantasy surveillance causing more harm to other people, by simple-minded people who assume, just because the officer is wearing a gun, he's OK? This experience, as well as the others in this writing, along with those stories and experiences aired on TV and radio, reveals the seriousness of the matter. I also thought that perhaps that these officers could have been having a public safety drill. This is what we do, try to over explain something away instead of dealing with what looks like a "red alert!"

This is just a real bizarre situation to get caught up in. Our worker thought and wondered how to protect herself in this type of scenario and if these in fact were police! As our worker began to leave Walmart, she looked for their store security to perhaps watch her as she walked to her car. Didn't find store security. Our worker thought that if these 3 people were having a real security work drill or imaginary delusion at our worker's expense, she did not want to become a part of their _imagined reality_. So our driver inquired at the Walmart service desk who could watch her as she walked back to her vehicle. www.cbc.ca; a CBS news story.

Now, how should our worker have looked at the situation? Was it a race thing because these 3 people that seemed to subtly be preoccupied with our worker were of a lighter complexion and our worker was of a darker complexion? Who do you suppose our worker could have safely reported this matter too? Could we suppose, potentially that the whole police station could be functioning like this? Could we wrap our head around this? We have whole families that could behave mentally challenged because "energies can transfer" in their environment! This drama seemed to be too bizarre to be considered a racial thing.

The stories could go on and on. Do you suppose our police have ever heard of the saying that some can become the actual work hazard? How would they know if no one reported what they were doing and/or if no one took seriously that our policemen could need help with their work realities? These particular incidences, as well as others, happened all in the year of 2015! Dear Lord, and this is August! My boss tells our driver whenever out, **"stay away from the police!"** Are we beginning to see that it does not seem to be a "race" thing! Also, I did wonder if any of these officers were on meds and perhaps the meds wore off. Also, we need to realize that if our officers are dealing with energies that could explain a lot, because energetic beings at certain levels are able to seize environments. You cannot ignore energetic spirit activity. These beings have a mission among us (an agenda and a course) and we need to understand this. Example: if these beings are manifesting, literally seizing our officers position during their line of duty, then our officers need to realize the need for them to learn how to resist the energetic being seized in their work environment because these beings **represent a** "dark spirit kingdom reality." And this is what I am seeing what is happening to our officers. I sure hope you understand what is being said in this writing. _Learn to resist the beings and stop letting them use you to wean out of our society those who do not want to serve them!_ *The more these energetic beings use you, the harder it will be to resist their dark spirit kingdom agenda. If our officers do not learn how to resist these energetic beings, what is to stop them from using our officers to rid our society of certain people groups, like these beings are using Muslim groups, Isis groups... any group who feels it is their job to show how much they hate and are intolerant of others. These groups express an energetic hate, a perpetual hate, that never ends.*

Some of our police officers are also found pulling certain darker cultures driving through their highways in Missouri over for traffic violations more so than lighter cultured drivers driving through the same area. Whether in any shopping location, Truck Stop facility, local gas stations, these types of surface "race" visual types of activities have not only been rising in the last few years, these types of incidences have been occurring consistently. Sandra Bland was pulled over for a minor traffic violation by a state trooper in Texas and was arrested, then found mysteriously dead in her jail cell. www.sandrablandtrafficviolation. www.tanishaandersonwhoclevelandpoliceslammedtothegroundinnovember.com

Then we have some civilians in society who want to retaliate against policemen for seemingly unfair injustices. However, we need to see there is a bigger picture. We assure you that these realities are being caused by energetic alien initiatives.  Please forgive me but I need to say that with the seemingly growing number of  innocent lives being taken, it would not be a biblical stretch to say that these innocent lives can be seen as sacrifices since they are being spearheaded by dark spirited energetic beings, according to Deuteronomy 19.2. Jeremiah 19.4. Jeremiah 2.34.

> "That innocent blood be not shed in thy land which the Lord thy God giveth thee for an inheritance, and so blood be upon thee ... Dt. 19.10"

## Marketing areas, Marketing ideas:
## Whether Internet or Movies

Seem geared toward desensitizing concerning ET types, revealing those creating the movies could be energetically effected in these types of industries. Evidenced by the media literature that comes out in a favorable light, concerning  accepting alien, ET beings. Again to deceive and cover up their true interest and initiatives.

They (those effected, without resistance) eventually take on the alien agenda (as their own). However, you can tell because it is not natural to think like the aliens but the transition and/or alien transformation becomes clear as the aliens continue their intruding visitations to process those they have selected. It is something to behold. How are we protecting humanity, one person at a time, from being alien processed and/or possessed. Whether in the home or in the marketplace, inter-net or movies, etc. Movies like "Limited less" shows us supernatural brain intelligence is possible, enhanced by a "pill."

It seems the aliens are finding more protection among us, as they continue to hide in and through-out our culture, community and society, via our bodies, images and/or imagination. And then using delusions and/or illusions when trying to enforce their agenda.  These beings are taking humanity by storm (or by accelerating rates) literally hiding behind and through people. They become another version of us by each soul they capture, but it is the manifestation of their work that is giving them away and we need to recognize that _what is happening among us is not being caused by us!_

## Sexual Choices, Sexual confusion: Galatians 3.28. 2 Tim 2.26

Happening or not happening among us, realized or not, are actually alien ideas, alien cre-ations. There are no "spirit/energy" genders. It is their influence and intention of simply being able to cause the confusion, while they feed off the confusion and the sin they cre-ate, it's what they do. Forgive me if this sounds to simplistic. Its just that as a society we really do not understand _spiritual kingdom activity_. We only seem to understand to some degree surface stuff (only things we can see). Yet the professional fields talk about things to explore, things you can't see and many unseen possibilities (yet they do not seem to have a problem visualizing. There are behaviors acting out among us that may point to something not seen, yet very present, happening among us. This can be caused deliberately by ener-getic intrusion to keep up the confusion and the "stupid" behaviors and seemingly mental mindless activities happening among us. Like people taking guns to church and taking out their (energetic) issues of frustration by the increase of deaths among us! This is the work of alien energetic beings that are able to seize the environment, fill the body, and take over the souls of men at will. Once they have processed a body of those WHO DO NOT KNOW HOW TO RESIST THEM!

No one really teaches how the energy of other worldly beings can effect us to the degree it needs to be understood. If we did perhaps more people would get saved, stay saved, and be more energetically kingdom-minded (less religious minded) and committed towards Christ and His cause among us. Just the reality that Christ is the _only_ kingdom that <u>offers salvation</u> is enlightening! The only One!

"We want things our way," can be an alien type mindset, which those constant thoughts turn into thinking patterns alien to truth. Jn. 14.6.

_"I am the way, and the truth and the life"_

Another reason that we are needing truth is that truth "even the truth of the words of Christ," also represents energy in itself. So then if we are looking at the energies of the both kingdoms, how is it possible to confuse the two? Both energy representations move in their own realities, regardless of if the vessels of mercy and grace realize this or not. This is why some people appear to be hypocritical and/or kind. Both energetic expressions "act" out or has its own expression! This is why **_a tree is recognized by its fruit, not by what the fruit wants to call itself_** nor by what its pretending to be. Jesus said:

"Either make the tree good and its fruit good or make
the tree bad and its fruit bad

# For the tree is known by its fruit."

Mt. 12.33. People who struggle with the fruit, making the fruit better etc., need to recognize and understand that they may be dealing with the energy either trying to express itself on or in their tree, so then we deal with the authority because energy represents one of 2 spiritual kingdom activities. Got it! Get it! Good! Once the energy can create the mindset in its subject as a pattern then the energy tries to come through the life ... to express its kingdom initiative and/or agenda as a kingdom expression. The biblical principle would be:

"as a man thinketh ..." Proverbs 23.7

Once we understand this, then it should not be hard to understand that righteousness is a **_greater energy,_** (no matter how wicked the wickedness is). Proof, it is righteousness that exalts a nation, not wickedness no matter how the wicked tries to promote energetic sin through wicked and evil agendas. _We say,_ <u>"excuse me, this is not about you."</u> We need salvation!

Therefore, when any nation is not being exalted for righteousness, there is a need to look at and then deal with the energy that is hindering and/or intruding upon its righteousness, (like the shedding of innocent blood, like protecting its borders, etc.,) because it is righteousness that promotes or exalts a nation! Now, can we see that God does not operate against Himself! God is righteous! Proverbs 14.34.

chapter 5

# Other Segments of Society and Categories that Beings also Seem to Master and/or Express Among Us

These beings also seem to be able to manifest, just pop up. Various places you go, you can likely see the same person showing up, until you begin to realize they seem to come from nowhere.

One of our workers stopped momentarily at a bus stop, when suddenly a person began speaking to our worker who was temporarily parked in that area, ready to take off, except this person began to ask for a ride, pleading that they had to get a ride. Well dear Lord, with a heart of compassion, our driver begins to take this person to the rapid station seemingly around the corner. Our driver asked this person if they wanted to go to the rapid station. When our driver tried to drop the person off, the person began to whine and whine stating that was not the place they wanted to go. OK. So our driver, listening carefully to the passenger, began to travel around the block and ended approximately where this passenger was picked up. Startled, our driver asked the passenger to please get out of the car. The passenger seemed disappointed that the ride was over but gave the impression they worked in the area. As soon as our worker dropped off the passenger and took off, our driver promptly looked in the rear view mirror and saw that the person was nowhere to be found. Driving away, our driver wondered if this was a real person or a real situation or was something trying to pull our driver into their reality.

A couple of days later, our driver parked in a local shopping area looked up suddenly and saw this person just standing there, as if they wanted a ride. Our driver gasped for breath and quickly looked the other way and took off, thinking "are you kidding me, how many times is this going to happen!"
www.educatinghumanityarepeoplereallybeingabducted.com

## Real Animals, *huh*!

We have seen bees seemingly with an agenda! Sounds funny but summer after summer, we have seen bees stay with certain drivers in the parking lot. But when others come around, you could break a sweat trying to find one!

It all seems to be a part of the "control" issue and process that these beings are constantly expressing and enforcing, when these beings are trying to attach to certain people, who are simply "not interested!" And so, we have seen these beings are able to influence and send:

- bees, to guard a persons door to harass the person getting out of a car and he person has to spray to get out safely … this can be a every day, all day, every summer thing! Nor do these bees die easy. Maybe some of these are hybrids too.
- we've seen the animal pestering with ravens that come out at night and continually walk upon the top of the vehicle but if you got out and looked you would see nothing! Nevertheless, this activity is inspired energetically.
- upon waking you may see a raven appear wherever you go for the day!

Yes, these beings are able to energetically operate through the animal kingdom, seemingly as another method of trying to get the attention of the subject or person they are interested in!

All this is happening in Ohio. Surely this kind of information could startle a psychologist who would wonder what kind of meds we have for hallucinations! But these are not hallucinations, these are *other worldly beings* with the potential and ability to break through time and space to connect with any of us and our world, with the ability to pull any of us into their reality!

We need to understand that these are actually happening now, that we need to learn how to deal with the energy engaging us. These are some of the things (realities) that energetic beings are desiring to pull men into, in order to help them capture the souls of men!

If we are witnessing this type of energetic activity happening among the animals, is it that difficult that they could find their way or push their way into the lives of men and use them to cause men to behave differently?

chapter 6

# What Does NASA
# Have to Do With It?

**NASA** is telling us in the Educational and Career Now.com article that they are taking students (or our space generation) and offering them the challenges of living and working in space and improving life on Earth. It seems that in the last 50+ years, our lives under alien activity, types of energetic manipulations of many areas of our humanity has not revealed that their activity has improved our personal relationships. We continue experiencing dishar-mony, not unity, due to the fact that our harmony and unity does not seem to be a concern of the aliens. Harmony in our humanity is not an alien DNA element. The daily culture and community disruptions that are making news is more revealing of alien intrusion work-ing behind the scenes. So how do we think that taking our children to another planet will improve our lives here? All I keep perceiving are alien agendas! They are the ones that were becoming extinct, not us. But, since their intrusions, everyone's health has been deteriorat-ing … seemingly from their personal interests in our bodies mentioned in this writing.

Does sending our children to another planet sound exciting to you? OK but at whose expense is this being done? And why isn't anyone ever speaking of any consequences whatsoever? Where is our spiritual intelligence?

Our research on alien space brother invasion revealed that the aliens did not end their research with our awareness at NASA nor with our US Army but has seemingly continued their steadfast energetic spirit work of intrusion into our society at the expense of our unity soundness (which includes our physical and spiritual well-being etc.).

During a time of negotiations, the space brothers (as energetic beings) seemingly with our permission (see internet article on "The Premise on Spiritual Warfare") shared and/or revealed information. What the alien space brothers did not reveal was that they had a hidden agenda, which was to see if they could breed with us (as a species). Once they found out that we were compatible, they would proceed to take certain people from our nation for experimental purposes (to try to engage sexually for developmental purposes of their kind). This would be without the permission of the people they took. Some are still being experimented on in their own homes by alien ritualistic type visitations. Simply because, everyone does not have the same energetic tolerance. It may take a bit more energetic ritualistic visitation to bring some into the place or position. It seems the aliens have the ability to pull any of us into a deep sleep and some are taken by this energetic method. Some times these beings can secretly pull you into a "sleep state" before you can call on the Lord! As a suggestion, we can set timers to check on ourselves throughout the night with a bottle of vinegar and water (and optional peppermint extract) to spray around us to break any energetic intrusive inconveniences. Some of us have someplace to be in the morning, other than another planet!

However, _you need to be just as serious and adamant about staying free_ from these beings attack on humanity, one person at a time, as the beings desire to capture our society, one person at a time. In Jesus name!

So it has been 50+ years now and these super beings (or alien space brothers) are continuing to move forward invading our individual lives, society and humanity. Finding ways to get and tax our psychic attentions and ability (as another energetic invasive method of pulling us into their reality and service to them).

People everywhere are finding or waking up with new aches and pains and/or memories or strange ideas, some of which come from the energetic beings trying to find a place to merge in the body and/or soul. These beings have evolved, surpassing devil only intelligence, by learning to turn their energy into matter (anything that takes up space) at a level by which they can intrude into our body(ies). These beings, light beings, have learned how to break through time and space just to connect with us. After the reference section of this book, you will find pictures of saucers coming from the sky to my RV when I was under ultra-red camera surveillance to find out why I could not sleep and why these beings try to control your sleep time. Getting Melatonin is just a good idea.

As in the book "The Dark Side of Cupid" revealed and I can confirm that the alien beings (ALSO REALIZED AS REPILIAN BEINGS) are not only up to no good, they represent a spiritual kingdom. If we would just listen, pay attention and look around and observe our society and communities we can realize that it is actually their work (their agenda) moving forward in our society (a society they evidently have decided to take at our expense) which is manifesting  harm, hate, division and danger. It is their DNA. It's what they do and in this respect, it is all they can bring to the table!

## There are only 2 spiritual kingdom activities operating among us. Only 2!

Milner, the CEO of a global investment firm (DTS Group), is spending the next decade seeking the sky for not only life (other life) but intelligent life, as they scan nearby stars, at least 100 galaxies, which may have their own planets. Milner calls his endeavor scientific marketplace with no foreseeable commercial purchase.

Milner speaks of SETI (Search for Extraterrestrial Intelligence, California based in 1984) whose telescopic reach is assisted by 9 million around the world who allow their computers to be used as a massive part that helps to distribute the network that processes SETI's data. Milner says what it took SETI 30 years to do he hopes his company, Breakthrough Listen, will do better.

Science can be a good thing. However, this article in "Time Magazine, 2015", also tells us about the 1970's when the twin Pioneer spacecraft launched that it carried plaques engraved with information that included startling things as:

- a map of earths location and
- a line drawing of a naked man and woman, revealing
- us to be the small, soft, *easy-to-eat creatures that we are!*

In light of what this writing is trying to accomplish, my first thought was:

## Are You Kidding Me?

This article goes on to say it made some people nervous! Are you telling me people in our nation, as well as other nations, are to suffer an excessive energetic activity because of the invitation of scientific research:

# Are You Kidding Me!

Milner tells us that Stephen Hawking, whom he calls a science icon, has expressed his doubts about the potential results of interstellar contact.

My second thought, after reading this article is:

# Unbelievable!

Holding back the tears at our potential level of ignorance that is effecting the world, here I am over 50 years later asking God what is happening in our society and why are we dealing with this excessive energy activity coming in the forms of aggravation, irritation and spiritual intrusion etc., only to find out that finding out seemed to be my assignment!

Energy with an assignment of which pictures reveal at the end of this writing how these energetic beings arrogantly contacted me! Who also began unveiling their potential negative energetic activity among us to attach to humans (by attacking some of us energetically) in an effort to not only process our bodies for use at their will and ill intention towards others but also to gain the ability to feed off or from our bodies nutrition while doing so. And now I read in the August issue of "Time Magazine" of a millionaire who wants to spend millions to find other intelligent beings. Rubbing my eyes, I'm thinking:

# Is this real!

Is anyone else getting this?

How many more of us have to be off of and drained daily of our nutritional existence to help with these over zealous (evidently effected scientist) projects.

Who is holding these scientists accountable? Who is protecting our nation from scientists with imagination seemingly beyond their intellect? But it is not beyond the intellect of these beings who are seemingly intelligent enough to use these scientists as a door into our nation to destroy our lives and society (from the inside out)! They continue to manifest trouble and division as their initiative among us as these beings are getting stronger and stronger!

What if this Milner, with his seemingly million dollar disaster potential, eventually if not already, contacts different beings who _are at odds_ with the ones evidently already here, evidenced by the growing John 10.10 scripture energy activity happening among us. Are we suppose to feed any other worldly planet out there whose existence is threatened and finds too that we are:

"Small, soft, **easy - to - eat** creatures that we are?"

Are we supposed to be likened unto a grasshopper in our scientists sight? Numbers 13.33. Were the majority of our scientists unbelievers or were there more atheists (alien influence) at the board table, who are allowing these types of ill-decisions to be made concerning our nation. We can get upset with President Obama for opening up our national borders but we have nothing to say to the scientist opening our spiritual borders. Why are our scientists seemingly siding with alien agendas instead of creating things to help protect us from their potential spiritual annihilation? Shouldn't our scientists be more spiritually keen and on guard and how is it many look to scientists as "god?" What kind of God feeds his people to their enemy – only those effected by the enemy, I assure you! How unsettling to say the least. I wonder if Trump would say, "YOU'RE FIRED!"

Does anyone feel like we are continuing to be "sold out?" What kinds of negotiations will this new set of scientists bargain with – our children? When people are spiritually energetically effected they simply can not hear any kind of warning! Their own scientist, Stephen Hawking, whom Milner called a science icon, had his doubts about interstellar contact. OK, so how do we intervene, in order to preserve the next generation? Are we going to continue to let any effected scientist behave as a sort of "god" over our nation.

*Is this our nation's destiny* – being crafted by alien beings deceitfully working and operating through our scientists causing us to be used as food for our enemies, who are being helped by our scientific quest for knowledge? Isn't there a tree of forbidden knowledge in the Bible that scientists are trying to tap into? Genesis 2-3. Are we even realizing that these energetic beings have the potential to put the thoughts and desires in the scientist in order to get them to a path that will help bring them into our reality, but as we are seeing hopefully, it is for their self-preservation!
O God,

## Where is our spiritual intelligence?

Nebuchadnezzar's "god" got so big in his imagination that he began to build his "god's" project as a golden image in the earth for the people to worship. Whoever did not bow down to worship this golden image would be thrown into the lion's den. Daniel, Chpt. 3.

# Summary

The article on the Charleston shooting in the "USA Today", June 19, 2015, issue speaks of strange church shootings and other shootings that involve or are initiated by Caucasians or by the lighter cultures engaging in violent type shooting sprees and other violent activities. What is interesting is that "USA Today" states that Hate Crime Statistics, reported by the FBI, say that in 2013, 5,928 hate crime incidences were reported. In 2012, 293,800 hate crimes were reported. The BJS (Bureau of Justice Statistics) study found that about 90% of hate crimes were violent and 60% were not reported, revealing the public is being mislead. However when a spiritually energetic work is operating, the activity (or deceit operating) can be hidden to anyone the energy is operating through. Why are the race crimes going unreported? What is really going on? Is there more of a spiritual aspect coming into play? Is it more likely an alien agenda is being carried out by energetic beings seizing and/or intruding into police activities? If so, these police are just as surprised as we are by what's happening among them. Are the policemen being used as a people group, like the other people groups, killing certain people or communities of people? Well how can we win a battle that we want to pretend doesn't exist or only effects some of us but not all? We need to get a grip as a society and put all our cards on "societies" table. How do you win a card game with half or three quarters of a deck of cards?

This article regarding the Charleston shooting goes on to say that there seems to be evidence of white supremacy patchwork activity but that now, the racist attacks seem to be more of a lone wolf profile style. It seems to be a sign that we could be dealing with (my version) "white supremist energies" or white supremists, because a predominantly African church was involved. It is also interesting, that I made mention that the same type or style of spirit activity that has been attacking Africa and keeping them down for so many years and that seem to keep division and strife going, even to the point of genocide, is now operating in our nation as found in the writing, "The Spiritual Root of the Matter is Found in Me". How could we possibly think to avoid genocide in our nation when we can't even openly discuss spiritual energetic hostile activity of alien beings who are spiritually forcing (by energetic means) their alien intrusive agenda upon humanity. By controlling levels of the body and souls of men using spirit energy domination, alien beings are causing men to be inhumane to men.

I thought that we were a nation that taught its inhabitants to be responsible. Yet we do not want to seem to go publically where everyone is, regarding the excessive spiritual energetic activity going on among us. Where did it come from and why and how it is effecting many on so many different levels? I don't even hear of anyone teaching on the subject as far as how to protect oneself from this, seemingly high level of bizarre, excessive spirit energetic activity. Does anyone else think this is strange? Does anyone care? Is anyone any longer capable of caring? Hopefully this writing can help us locate ourselves and help preserve our souls so that we can gain the ability to see how to make our way through with the help of the Lord. Psalms 46.1.

Should we still continue to handle the surface problems we can measure with meds, with horse and buggy type remedies, while we prepare our students to go to the moon? What is wrong with this picture? See the June, 2015 issue of, *Media Planet Magazine* at www.educationandcareernews.com

Can we discuss that alien abduction activity could be the cause and/or continuing spiritual warfare of many. Or is this too sensitive a subject for those who have already been spiritually effected (or spiritually conditioned or energetically dominated by the alien activity and agenda)? Isn't this part of our dilemma or concern for at least 50 years now? How much longer do we have to continue walking around with people that are spiritually energetically <u>unsafe?</u> Giving you the impression that if they are spiritually effected, against their will (spiritually dominated), then so should everyone else be? Can we wrap our heads around the idea that some people <u>are</u> this effected?

> It is not spiritual to be negatively spiritually effected. It is a disease. So there is a need to retrain our societies and communities on how to deal with negative energy intrusions. When we learn to rise up and deal with the energy that many evidently did not know how to protect themselves from and so these beings continue to break through the centuries when they can, and try to rebirth their sin and iniquity. It's all they can bring to the table. Jn. 10.10.

The earth was given to man and we need to rise up and deal with the energy that is not only trying to tear our lives but also humanity and society apart and then proceed to taking our children's lives. We can break this demonic culture *if there is enough of us sound enough* to. O God please help us hold on to our blessings in the earth (the earth that you have given to men), in Jesus name!

Some are so spiritually effected they really do not know how to ask for help. Where can they go without someone wanting to put them on meds? We have people who can't go to work everyday, without someone who has been spiritually effected, that darkness forces (spiritual forces) use (people as vessels) to spiritually energetically effect someone else before they go home, until the targeted person becomes spiritually dominated by continual energetic intrusions into the body and/or the soul.

**Where** can people go to stop others from spiritually trying to effect them without losing their job or risk being put on meds ( often of no real understanding of what is spiritually going on in our world) because they do not want to be spiritually entrapped by an employee who spiritually could be? We are living in a society that is not considering all that people have to deal with. We are literally forcing people to be spiritually subject and/or spiritually contaminated by those who evidently are? Why we are seemingly allowing this? Is it ignorance or fear or both? Are you kidding me? Doing nothing does not seem to work for us – look how far its brought us so far. www.thepremiseofspiritualwarfareinrelationtoalienabductions.

According to research, while psychologists were hypnotizing clients to find out what the aliens were doing, it seems that whatever accumulation of information was being formulated that our army personnel and/or scientists continued to publically resist the possibility of life activity elsewhere besides earth (or so it was said). Yet even today we find radio announcers such as Clyde Lewis on KXL, located in Portland Oregon picked up by a station in Columbus, Ohio interviewing someone like Captain K (Randy Cramer/Captain Kaye) discussing "Ground Zero." www.captainkofmars/groundzerowithclydelewis.com.

This conversation spoke of Captain K's experiences on Mars. Captain K tells us he spent 17 years at a secret Mars military base and how there are 2 main indigenous species on Mars. He tells of how he was posted to the Red Planet to recruit military personnel from other countries as well as the U.S. www.marsdisclosure:moremarsrecallofrandycramer/captaink.com, www.whistleblowerrandycramertellsaboutsecretmilitaryoperations.com.

How they and our business industry have made such advancement that they are trying to pass a bill to protect space mining operations and manufacturing on Mars. I believe this announcer wants to continue this interesting topic so that more people become aware of how far advanced we are. Their listener's phone number presently is 712-432-2854. Live Stream, Mon-Fri, 7 pm-12 midnight, Pacific on WCRS-LP, Columbus Community Radio. www.wcrsfm.org. This program aired in July, 2015.

What is also interesting is that this guest, Captain K, also mentioned a type of war (evidently spiritual/energetic war) or battling among certain "beings" on Mars for territory there. Also one of the beings battling or warring was of a reptilian type nature which seems to be a very militant type being. _This is one of my points_: those evidently being spiritually effected in our nation, by these reptilian beings will also, as we are seeing among us, actually be taking on a militant type of energetic spirit nature (to the degree one is effected and/or taken over by them). This is why our police and/or those effected by these beings, including those who rise up against police in retaliation, are symptoms of those changing before us, becoming more militant because they are taking on these beings spirit natures. Mainly, I believe it's because no one that I have found is teaching how to resist these beings and are thereby becoming spiritually/energetically effected by them. The way our officers are being effected is being revealed right before our very eyes – as a type of hostility against certain cultures in our community (the black or darker natured inhabitants). So is the concern leadership. No it is spiritual, backed up by an alien agenda concerned about the survival of their species. That is to say, you cannot ignore dark spirit activity happening among us, concerning a soul, neither can you remedy it with only meds. Are we saying that we can't see the bigger picture until all of society is on meds?

Often you may run into those in allegiance with these negative energies, either one of a different culture, in a different neighborhood or visa versa or sometimes with those in their own neighborhood. It does not matter to negative energetic activity, they only want a body to express their negative energy through. They will sit in their vehicle until the random subject is chosen by alien entity energy operating through inclination or surge of energy upon certain parts of the body. Then they begin to give silent commands to their subject like "get out of the car" or "look at me." This could very well be done by what they call a non-religious person doing this to a perhaps more like religious subject (we are dealing with energies of two different spiritual kingdom activity – one who already owns or created the earth and the other trying to take possession of it) just because they can. I asked the Lord "how is this possible for non-believers to give these types of spiritual commands" when we (as believers) have authority in Jesus name? They do it by energetic accumulation.

What I have come to realize is one of the reasons the energies are trying to penetrate everyone they can is because it opens up their second realm over the subjects penetrated. So that when a person is in allegiance with an energy (or is being used as prey by the energy) over a certain territory and the energy wants to pull a person deeper into a level of their energetic realm, they will have the one in allegiance begin to command a subject to look at them or come to them (it can get tricky here). It seems the subject does just what the person in allegiance to the energy wants. If this is happening in your area and/or the enemy's territory, then you want to keep or create a flow chart. as a potential <u>energetic tool of faith</u> (without faith it is impossible to please God). Whenever you need to go into this seemingly spiritually contaminated area walk around with the flow chart and do your business silently releasing any negative energy concerning you, in you, or around you. Even do this while you are standing in line to make a purchase anywhere and until you are pretty much out of the area. You are on a faith assignment to get through the territory free and then get back home free. So, as you go through really any territory, fold up your flow chart in 4 sections as you go and softly or silently say "Lord, I am resisting any negative energetic activities around me in Jesus name." I resist, _____ _____I resist it _____I resist it. In the blank spots are the names on the flow chart you are saying to resist the dark energy around you in any territory, it may even be in your home. This faith tool can even keep you out of an <u>energetic argument </u>(that can quickly arise from energetic beings coming or seizing the environment, similar to what our officers are dealing with) because when those energies flow and the gods come on the scene, they will try to work from anyone's aura realm. They cannot if you are speaking the authority words of Christ to resist the energies around you. I have and do this while waiting at the drive thru for food and it keeps me out of those energies residing in those areas <u>looking</u> for prey and/or expression. So, keep the word ready in your mouth, when you leave the house until you get home. This is how the Lord can keep us through and with His word. Ps 108.12. Ps 31.3. The word works when YOU work with it. So, let's give the Lord something to work with for this is the reason He came to destroy the works of the enemy. Now can we see clearer Lord, in Jesus name. Thank you. Amen. 1Jn.3.8.

> Is it just me or are others noticing that the "gods" seem to express racism, division, confusion and disharmony by the activity they are causing among us and those they are able to express themselves through? It is here we can realize that spiritual release is needed? Hopefully, we can also see that these need to learn how to protect (and/or spiritually release) themselves from how energetic beings would use them and/or express hate and disharmony through them.

Also, especially ministers of our God, keep a bottle of vinegar/water/peppermint mix when you are driving, or any combination that works for you, so when the energy comes to pull you into a sleep while driving to cause a accident, not only open the windows a bit but spray almost continually.

A minister passed away in Akron, Ohio. He turned his car over while driving at night. Some mistakes we can't afford to make! Please pray. www.akronpastordiedincarcrashmay,2015.com

***One of our immediate goals, when dealing with any level of alien intrusion, is to hold onto our lives in Christ and His will and purposes for our lives*** (which would include our humanity). One way to do this, besides maintaining our spiritual connection, condition and relationship with Christ, (because the aliens' intentions are to use any of these alienist invasive options and initiatives, some of which are listed in this writing) is to first distract and then sever your relationship with Christ and others usually in your environment including your family. This idea could traumatize you all by itself. Community needs to recognize when energetic beings are trying to keep people out of the Lord's fold or inheritance (and there are energetic assignments to do just this continually). It is usually the one gifted to some level of healing and/or understanding the body, hopefully through the church system that recognizes this. However, when the church system is warred against, this can be very challenging and/or difficult to say the least because the gift and what is offering to the Lord is still needed, despite the level of battle they could be dealing with. So let us recognize that the Lord, as Administrator of His gifts, is able to work the gifts needed outside the church back into the church, and the churches of God are encouraged to keep looking for the gifts of God which are needed and are a part of the operations of God in the earth and heaven. Bless the Lord who is not without witness in that He is good! Acts 14.17. Corin.12.

As we learn how to protect our bodies from alien intrusions and captivity, we'll then be able to maintain our souls in Christ. Having a book bag with the items listed in this writing could prove useful and convenient, (or anything you sense might work better in your circumstance, this is a place to seek the Lord if anything else is needed), when we are being inconvenienced by alien intentions which always seem to manifest when we have any business to take care of us and/or simply relax. So when they come with their drama to try to distract your day and your life, learn to take the time to resist with what works for so that you can go on with your plans. Learn not to be discouraged by the enemy, just keep pressing your way, you will find that the Lord will show up in battle, as you call upon His Name!

So pace yourself and learn to run this race with patience, in Jesus' name. Learn how to resist alien frustrations with prayer (on the spot, quietly to yourself, or softly out loud). I can only imagine that the Lord spared my life to be a witness to those with ears to hea. The Lord is faithful.

# Above all remember this, which could also prove useful to our armies, that even though energy cannot be destroyed … it can be reformed … refashioned … and

# Diluted

to lessen any penetrated effect which could present an advantage in any battle.

We need a U.S. army that can potentially understand that the one and true living God had all the answers they needed for their existence. We only need to search for those seeking the Lord (in relationship with the Lord). Why would we look elsewhere?

So I pray this information reaches our armies also. We need not fear the aliens but we do need to know how to resist them in Jesus' name simply because aliens seek to expand their kingdom. When alien forces try to penetrate our army forces with their energy, figure out how many instruments are needed to dilute their energy in Jesus name (using water and/or water and vinegar) . Please remember to say "thank you" for the Lord is able to help us, even when we miss it. For the Lord is not without witness in that He does good.

Lord, I pray for America that You would keep Your eyes on her (us) still, one person at a time, one family at a time, one church at a time, one nation at a time, for all is Yours. You are the reason why we are here. We need You still. To show forth Your glory. How marvelous and perfect …

chapter 7

# Communion

The Lord still makes himself available for those who will take the needed time and perhaps necessary to wait in the presence of the Lord. Even those seeking healing and release from things in common with the serpent, including snake bites (spiritually and naturally so). We see in scripture that Paul had a lifestyle with communion and communing with the Lord, even when the ship he was on wrecked, right before the viper bit him on the Island. Acts 28.

Some say perhaps we should be having communion more often, due to a seemingly growing need among us. Is it possible to have communion more often, not for religious reasons, but to help keep us more focused on prayer, healing and the need to be in the Lord's presence. The Bible reveals that Jesus would be eating with the brethren and then go right into communion according to Matt: 26.26

> And as they were eating, Jesus took bread, and blessed it, and broke it, and gave it to the disciples, and said, take, eat; this is my body.

Taking communion more often seems to reveal more about not only our need for Jesus, but about life with Jesus. After all He did say,

> Verily, verily, I say unto you, except ye eat the flesh of the son of man and drink his blood; ye have no life in you.
> Jn. 6.53. Corin. 11.23-26.

## All roads still point to Jesus!

The only God that offers salvation. Relationship, not religion!
Jn. 14.6. Rom 10.9-10. Titus 2.11.

chapter 8

# Acting Like Aliens Don't Exist is Not Working for Us!

### It's in the statistics, people!

*What kind of battle for the soul is this*? When your enemy can cause those they abduct, for seemingly selfish reasons, to eventually befriend ***them because*** even while the alien beings are causing family and friendship splits and divisions; to keep you entrenched with their distraction(s) and enslaved to the alien's initiatives (which could include a new partner, drugs, untimely deaths, police and/or racial tension and conflict, political conflict yes, and even homosexuality is being used among us; *it's what the aliens do*, then they feed off of it (the chaos they are creating among us) as it will also cause them and their intensions to grow and go forward among us! ***Please don't think it's all about you,*** it's about **"sin"** people. Which can be (and is) a spiritual thing, especially when it is coming out of a spiritual realm and agenda until **we** learn how to resist it according to James 4.7. It is not as much as a political issue as it is an alien agenda (they are the ones that really have no gender issues to quibble over). The concern is that we are **not** understanding how much they are operating among us. To the degree that mass murders are happening among us; to the degree homosexuality seems like a issue among us; to the degree it seems our policemen are struggling with justice issues in the midst of civil unrest (that if truth be told, they are creating, and then they run to the situation as if they know nothing about it). What are you talking about sister? I am saying there are days when I go to the local park, just to walk exercise, and within 15 minutes time an officer shows up because now our parks are videotaped. Then I leave the park because of the issues with the policemen, who wants to be around those who seemingly are on psychic patrol. Yep, so I leave the park and go a couple of blocks to a local store to buy shoes and as I am preparing to get out of my vehicle this same police mysteriously shows up around the *Lakewood/Cleveland* area. He parks about 2 car lengths from me and I am in their rear view mirror! Should I yet feel uncomfortable? That was May 7, 2015.

The day before, early in the morning around 7-9 o'clock am, I stopped at the local Willoughby Target store off I-90 and Rt. 91 and all is well. I run in to get paper towels and I pay for my items then go to my car. I decided at that moment to put a piece of paper towel in my shoes to make them more comfortable. As I put on my right shoe, I noticed a white van suddenly parked 2 car lengths before me before me in a strange manner and did not get out of the vehicle. As I preceded to put a piece of paper towel in my left shoe, suddenly another marked police car parks at a angle off to the left a bit. This police officer squares me off and just mysteriously sits there facing my way and I am thinking "are you kidding me!" … As I wondered what was going on, it seemed this was another area the police were surveying with a video. OK, I was not the only person leaving but I noticed I was the only black person leaving the store at this particular time. So you can't help wonder, is this what their surveillance is for? Are they not concerned with giving this impression? What is going on? I immediately leave, going past what could have turned out to be an episode if I had not left. I go straight to the gas station (Speedway) around the corner on Rt. 91 and call the local Willoughby police station to ask to speak to who is in charge of these officers and their strange behavior! Of course, I got the answering machine and no one called me back. I would encourage anyone dealing with strange police in their neighborhood to start logging whenever they encounter the same policemen throughout the day, day by day. Get their police number, time and date and when you call the police station and they do not return your call. Find a lawyer and show him what you have been logging and let them deal with the officers.

This needs to be done due to the growing alien intrusions among us. We keep telling society if you see something strange tell it. But if the strangeness is coming from those who are supposed to keep us safe? They make a law and tell us it's not legal to say what the police do or what is your proof. OK, then how do we uphold the laws of the land when our police officers are so spiritually/energetically effected? Our police officers need to learn how to also deal and with alien energies plaguing communities across the land just like everyone else. Everyone is responsible for what they are doing or allowing. If they don't know how to deal with it so I guess then it's OK to be a part of the problem! Forgive me for putting this incident in this writing but this may be my only justice and legal record of the account. Do you know how startling it is to BE PUT in this position and it could have went south. This was NOT the first time this happened to me at this location, it was only the first time this year! OUR Police Officers need help! They do not know how to resist dark spirit energies that represent a kingdom trying to rise among us. They need to be taught just like the rest of us! They are NOT exempt. It is not fair that those who are spiritually effected and in these examples becoming unsound in their civil duties. When they are becoming the problem to have the authority to arrest us for their spiritual issues! Look, in Jesus name I have the authority to say this. It's my job! I got God on my back, if I don't do this. God hears the cries and sees the injustices. So to God be the glory when righteousness and justice meet!

## This is the degree that the alien being influence is among us.

This is the bigger picture. The concern is that the Bible teaches us to rule among our enemies. But many are being continually energetically affected. Some don't know what to do. Others are becoming menaces to society because the enemy is using them in private sector jobs. Literally flowing energy through them to attack others by filling the bodies with excess energy. Whom the alien would not be able to attack in such a way, unless he uses someone his subject host can get close to. In this way, forcing people off their jobs (unless they want to keep their job only by getting effected) because our society offers no other help than meds. But they don't want to seemingly bother with those the enemy is using as a vessel or tool to pressure others into receiving negative energy. This too, will be added to our list as a cause for homelessness. Women are getting pressured out of their homes because the alien energies will not let the man rest until he has troubled the family and the family is confused because the man is supposed to protect the home. The problem is not the man. It's that no one is dealing with alien manifestation trying to press its way through the family! So, yes there is a need for people to learn how to discern and then resist hostile alien energetic activity. So that no one can be made to be a spiritual victim (through a series of physical maladies) and/or not be used to help make others alien subjects. Whether one wants to work (secretly or openly or not) against anyone is not the issue. It is, however, an alien agenda and if all they have to do is get that negative energy in you to do so, what's going to stop them? <u>Not ignorance!</u>

People are attacking others because they are being attacked (spiritually energetically attacked) so are our police officers.

As Christians we have authority but we need to learn how to, as the Bible says, "rule among our enemies." Paul had authority but he still had to work to make a living. Otherwise, we have dormant authority. How can you use your authority if the enemy is making or causing your sickness and creating your disease? Yet, it is in the statistics what the enemy has and is continuing to try to do! How can we rule unless we understand how we can protect and preserve our body, soul, spirit (and thereby society) from excessive energy activity? This is not a race thing, not a police thing, gender thing … this is a "kingdom thing!"

## Why, *<u>RULE AMONG OUR ENEMIES!</u>*

Because Jesus paid a great price for our freedom, why would we want or allow ignorance to be our defeat? Why because the earth belongs to men? There is <u>not</u> scripture where God gave the earth to aliens over His children and that is why there was battle in the other worlds. The earth belongs to men. It doesn't matter if aliens were able to deceive our army and scientists, which seemed to be the "open door" for the aliens to walk and/or operate in this nation according to research! How is it we can get upset with Obama for opening up the borders to earthly foreigners (and not even make sure their health conditions will not effect our kids?); but not get upset with our scientists and/or army communities for allowing aliens to come through the borders of our space realm and give them place in the science community, with a hidden agenda to spiritually compromise us; and behave spiritually and energetically hostile and jeopardize our security, homeland peace; our health is being deteoriated, mental statistics are rising, they attack the nerve system (peripheral nervous system, while creating the causes of suicide). They can attack sometimes daily because we are dealing with an

# Army of Aliens!

Hebrews 11.35

It is the energetic activity (i.e. symptoms, constant ill-attitude(s) of consciousness directing

chapter 9

# Energy is Energy People
## The Fall

Its ill energy towards you, in the form of: opposing views/attitudes/forces and/or intruding energies that try to climb into your private body areas each night ... signified by the ache/pain/shame and offense of whatever alien energies or who they send are doing ... in an effort to sustain their life as energetic beings/while trying to pull you into their dark spiritual kingdom realm of activities (of distraction/sin/sickness/perversion/unrest/deceit, etc;) and, at the same time, pull you out of the true God's path for your life.

Another way of explaining this invisible energy activity concept (that our alien beings are using or operating in, as it presses its way to find greater places in our lives) that can effect us behaviorally, physically and energetically, by their energetic intent or means of expression, is by looking at and understanding how the Earth (as Gaia) operates by moving through energy, energetically through the earth element itself, or through fire elements, water, wind and storm elements. Gaia, as an expression, does not take the place of God, it only explains the earth's ability to function energetically (and God is in all things, Ps. 57.2, Gen 1.): This hypothesis explains that:

Our planet functions as a single organism that maintains conditions necessary for its survival.

That the health of the Earth is always revealed as a dynamic state, always balancing itself between these elemental forces.  Likewise, the mind, body and spirit can be grouped into 5 categories:

-physical, energetic, emotional, mental and spiritual and any of these categories that become off balanced can effect us.

God created ... and saw that it was very good ..." Gen 1.

*An organism is a form of life composed of mutually interdependent parts that maintain their various vital processes.

## **The Analogy:** The Fall

In the "fall," the angels (as energetic spirit beings) left their first estate and biblically represent the only other spiritual kingdom that exists, the first being the kingdom of God. The "fall" of these angel spirit beings could also represent their character as seemingly off-balanced biblically in comparison to the Christ biblical character.

- "and his kingdom was full of darkness"

- "love does not behave itself unseemly, seeks not her own, not easily provoked, thinks no evil."

- "angels kept not their first estate …" Jude 1.6

- "and their place was found no more in heaven" Rev 12.8

Those fallen angels that, operationally, over time have learned how to not only reinvent themselves, but also how to break through time and space (our space) realm to gain the ability to effect others they come into contact with in the earth, in negative ways (no matter the initial deceit nor intent) because that is all they can bring to the table, the fruit of Jn 10.10. Likewise, those they eventually are able to effect in the Earth will seem to evolve into their character because these energetic beings have learned how to merge (or release their energy) into humanity to try to reform them and/or replace the lives of humans with what they call human hybrids and/or alien hybrids, depending on their subject's position taken! Those souls have not learned how to resist their energy. Some have not even learned that they are supposed to resist them (and there are too many opinions concerning the matter). People really need to understand, saved or not, there is a need to resist these beings because they are perverse, no matter how they are able to reinvent themselves in any generation. I am not sure why this seems to be a hard concept to teach – the difference between 2 spiritual kingdom activities among us, only 2, and how to hold onto the only kingdom that offers salvation in the Earth, Jesus. Parents, do you understand? I am truly sorry if anyone missed this, but please, can we help save the next generation? Pastors, there is a need to ask the Lord how to preach and minister to alien subjects. Because many are not strong enough in their faith to resist the alien beings who are hanging around – some day and night as watch guards, to make sure they don't read their Bible, make sure they are confused about some … just constantly trying to lock in their mindset to second realm activities. I mean sometimes I need to drive an hour or two out of the city just to find a quiet place to read my Bible. I realize many cannot do this, so how are you ministering to alien subjects among us? This is serious.

- these fallen beings are causing others to sin, because they embody sin (or darkness) as fallen beings. Rev 16.10

- and is why they cause in the lives of those they try to capture, or of whose lives they try to become a part of, sin and iniquity and is the reason it is necessary to learn to resist these fallen energetic beings … Isa 5a9.2. These fallen angel beings do not entertain grace, nor do they regard it (the Lord's operation, nor His administration) Ps 28.5, Corin 12.5. These aliens, whether invisible or operating within humanity, break up homes, break up unity or harmony wherever it is found, as well as relationships. They literally feed off ill-emotions that they help to create and there are no demonic graces in their repertoire. James 4.7 Jere 10.10.

We must learn how to safeguard our relationships in Christ (this would include learning how to resist dark spirited energetic activity invisibly operating or whether through a person). We need to understand that we do have the ability in Christ, to withstand alien agendas but we need to learn from those God has revealed how so we don't lose our faith and take it personally and think that God doesn't care, when He does!

With this said, just because we can't always physically see how the Earth is moving through or by elements, we can see its operation when it's manifest through either the fire, water, storm and earth element itself. It's how God created things. He created all things! He is a God of purpose. Ecc 3.1

"Thou sendest forth thy Spirit, they are created."   Ps 104.30

chapter 10

# Scenario

## My People Perish for Lack of Knowledge
## Proclamation
## Pastor
## Book Reference
## Author Page
## Pictures

Scenario, *live examples and episodes (shared by others and/or experienced) for us to learn or conceive <u>how</u> we can biblically recognize goings on as activities, some seemingly inno-cent, but need to be resisted in order to not give place to our energetic spirit enemy's agenda (working within and among our cultural experiences). Simply because our energetic alien spirit beings are looking for places of expression in our day-to-day living experiences, as well as places within or about our body, soul and spirit lives. James 4.7. People, just stay with me! <u>There are many levels of dark energetic spirit operations going on among us</u>. Some people are literally being haunted by these beings … and the beings can literally use those that have been spiritually affected as bait to pull anyone that is being targeted into any energetic spirit beings reality simply by causing trouble in a person's work or home environment (or even create or cause trouble wherever the targeted person or subject goes)! Yes, it appears with observation these energetic spirit beings, which represent a spiritual kingdom, are using the workplace as a sort of place to spiritually train and indoctrinate men into their service realm activity as an operation.*

*We need to wrap our heads around this because, others may need us to recognize they are not the problem but the problem can just come on the scene and act out (via energetic spirit activity, through humanity, one person at a time). By creating confusion, disharmony, etc., is also a way these beings can literally feed off the energy of men and get stronger! This brings the power of truth into play; resist the devil (the darkness, the negative energy, the bad attitude, wrong thoughts, and the wrong or unbiblical thinking patterns, the unkindness, etc …) because it is NOT ALL ABOUT YOU!*

"And there was war in the heavens and Michael fought with the dragon, and the dragon
was cast out that old serpent called the devil … and he was cast out into the earth and
his fallen angels …" Mt 25.41. Ps. 37.22.

But they are trying to make it about their energetic spirit ability to spirit force you even through
others among us that may be easier to get to submit, lure or deceive due to biblical illiteracy (even
on your job they are spirit training men collectively to wait on them 2Tim.2.26), to draw on their
negative spirit energy collectively as a force and literally aim this spirit energy at those the energetic
beings have decided not to include in their dark energetic spirit agenda (which are usually those
with Christ light. It doesn't matter if this means a person has to lose their job and their ability to
make a living, perhaps because you (the fearful and deceived) decide not to be used by these dark
energetic spirit beings. Sometimes it is easier to point the finger at others to get the attention off
of us. Then these employees (or hidden leaders help create a dark camp among you, these spirit
you into dark ways, attitudes that fit in with dark spirit initiatives – some are considered "plants"
of darkness, operating among us, brought into your work environment, if they aren't already there,
usually in place of a saint or the saint is then conveniently removed, driven out by secret penetrations that ail the body) are then able to cause fellow employees to collectively draw on these
negative spirit energies who then go to church on Sundays. No one realizing at church this person
or people are being "spirit forced" to draw on these negative energies on their job collectively. Each
day the people grow stronger in this dark spiritual indoctrination activity happening among them.
You then, bring them into church to energetically attach to subjects in the church to continue their
"spirit agenda" and the pastor becomes spiritually blind-sided at first, not realizing that someone
among them is willing or spirit forced to participate on their job with darkness. They are probably
being used energetically or prophetically as an instrument to transport this dark energetic spirit
activity into our church system. Who is teaching otherwise because most don't want to go there?
Hello! We are already there! Job 36.21. Eze. 18.24. Mt. 13.41. This is happening because men
would rather submit and be pulled into these dark energetic spirit activities than lose their jobs
**because having a job or not is their reality.** So this is where ministry and message of Christ is
needed, where Christ becomes real. Who is preaching on this reality – how to live without comfort,
while darkness is taking or trying to take your place and/or how to submit your soul to hellish spirit
activity on your job, so you can feed your family? However, the ironic choices become forms of
energetic spirit design(s) of entrapment where men are found to be the cause of others to lose their
jobs than to be without a job. This was done quickly. So men are being energetically pulled (when
these energetic beings come to their jobs) into negative or ill-energetic religious spirit activity on
their jobs lures excess energies in and gives them a place not only in their lives but in the lives of
others through harmful ways because the energetic spirit beings are weaning out people on our
jobs, in our communities and societies, even in some of our churches (by many of the ways listed in
this writing) …

## Example 1

3 women walk into a restroom of a nice store that we will call (T). When they walk in, one after another, there
is already a woman in there washing her hands. One of the women that walks in is of a darker culture than
the rest. Two of the lighter cultured women came out and the woman that was already in the restroom, whom
you thought was leaving, for some reason was still there washing her hands seemingly now in the way and
everything is getting congested. Anyway, the 3rd woman comes out of the stall (the darker cultured woman)
and this 3rd woman, who seemingly was in the stall next to the darker cultured woman comes out and
"feels" the urge to ask everyone "does anyone sense a strong smell?" Well immediately, the darker cultured
woman recognized the "energetic personality" trying to find a place to come through, that this woman was

manifesting; and the darker cultured women, due to the comment thought it best not to wash her hands, even though washing hands is a good thing to do; it was definitely not the right time! Now a day it seems easy to get pulled into the excess energy of others. There was a time when some marveled because Jesus had not washed His hands. Lk 11.38-43. So we see, that some, whether in the church or out of the church, can behave indifferent to others. Sometimes being around others that are manifesting can cause their energy to transfer. Galatians 5.19-21 reveals other possible negative manifestations.

Questions:

Does anyone think anything was implied here?

Did the darker cultured woman do the right thing?

Do we think this person was acting in love by an unkind implication? Gal. 5.19-26.

Did this woman use this comment to distinguish the different cultures in the restroom to point out their differences?

Isn't the bathroom the place where one can expect smells?

Did lighter cultured women feel the need to discuss the topic of smell in the rest room to strangers?

*It was apparent that the other women had not noticed any smells.*

*Do we think maybe the smell could have been a strange type of loving revelation to this woman? Rom. 13.10.*

*Why didn't the lighter cultured women leave also?*

*How did the other women become swayed and stay?*

Did the lighter cultured women feel the need to stay and maybe support each other, if so why, just because there was a different culture there? Perhaps if there is fear.

*Just because no one came in with a crystal ball does not mean there was no energetic activity happening? There is an indication that this woman, with the seemingly smell manifestation that thought she needed to share, was being moved or motivated by negative energetic activity which is a spirit kingdom activity that supports the work of a darker rather than a lighter kingdom activity. (Job). So the light she received was from the operation of darkness that loves to point out differences, unkindnesses, and disharmony (due to excess energy spirit drama). What is sad is that she seemed to be able to draw the other women into this negative energetic activity. Do we think children could also be effected by this negative energetic expression or activity?*

*We need to recognize this energetic type of spirit activity as either negative or positively intended (if not by the person, then by the energy that has found a place to operate through this woman's life to effect others; because apparently she is already effected, since it seems to be making itself a part of the other women's experiences; otherwise energetically, it (the spirit in operation) points to the grace of God, or demi-gods its forcing its expression in this woman experience and now able to influence others! Eph. 4.27. 2Tim. 2.26.*

# Example 2

*There was a darker cultured woman in line at the register to pay for her purchases at a store called (T). Shortly after which, a lighter cultured woman stands behind the darker cultured woman, with her son behind her. Quickly, it seemed for no apparent reason, this woman's son walks around his mom (who came up to his mother's waist for height) and stands between his mom and this darker cultured woman. He then looks at the darker woman and whispers to his mom, "something smells."*

*This is important to recognize because energetic beings operate territorially, which means they need to first satiate the energetic spirit personalities of those they are trying to operate through (their subjects) and the way you can begin to perceive what is going on and/or which spirit kingdom is developing at any given time. You know them by their fruit. Mt.12. When you go to different places and different people are seemingly expressing the same things, you are seeing energetic spirit manifestations with the territory, with the ability to follow you, if assigned to you. Usually to try to spook you and/or simply let you know they are there. This is why some of the people they effect, seemingly take on their spirit personality, become suspicious. Being continually suspicious of others reveals one needing some level of spiritual release and this is also a good place to minister among us. Being continually suspicious of other cultures or any one person you feel is not like you is not normal behavior. Giving grace and compassion used to be considered normal behavior and is still the measuring rod to reveal if God's Spirit energy is operating or not. If not, surely this is where Bible study is needed, to work nicely while one is working on releasing (same as resisting in a sense) themselves from negative spirit energies. James 4.7. The writing,* **_The Spiritual Root of the Matter is Found in Me,_** *can explain more on how to energetically release oneself, by faith, for without faith it is impossible to please God. Heb. 11.6.*

You want to gain the ability to recognize the personalities (energetic spirit being are personalities) but you don't want to get sucked into them. How? Words (like the energetic spirit thoughts which they try to project onto us) can and do carry energy. So, when they are able to get someone enticed by their bait as soon as the conversation begins, the energetic beings can begin to flow and can manifest (or grow) in the conversation, which can make it difficult to stop. If we can leave the area quickly (if not pull our or your own scripture flow chart through and focus on Christ energy and He will come on the scene and show up or manifest in our hearts where we hide His word) with a smile in our soul because people are important, we can, like Peter said, save ourself!  Acts 2.40. Gal. 5.19-16. Ps 91.3.

"He whose mind is stayed on Thee is kept in perfect peace ..."  Isa 26.3.

<u>Example 3</u>
Another example tells us of a darker cultured woman (Christian woman) goes into a library in northern Ohio. <u>After about an hour to 2 hours</u> or so (as if someone was awakening), suddenly a policeman walks by (passing by those who were having a seemingly loud conversation). He then walks past the darker cultured woman, as he seems to be going about his rounds about the library. Between the rows of library books there was a clear isle that leads to where a darker cultured woman was quietly sitting by a window. Suddenly, slowly coming down between the rows of books, down the clear isle of where the darker cultured woman was reading her book, was a lighter cultured woman who seemed to have a position in the library because of her clothing and because there seemed to be around 3 or 4 lighter cultured girls with her, staying closely around her. As they all walked down this clear row about half way down of the rows of books they seemed to huddle themselves. At a particular row of books, that was in the clear isle, a little ways before, where the darker cultured woman was. What got the darker cultured woan's attention was that, out of her peripheral view, while still trying to read, she (the darker cultured woman noticed this group of ladies walking down this clear isle before her), but as the woman stopped in this clear isle before her and then positioned themselves in a type of huddle with the ladies who were with her, the darker cultured woman continued trying to read; but could not help notice out of her peripheral view that, not only did this group of women stop before her, the darker cultured woman began to wonder why seemingly this group of women

seemed to be preoccupied with her. This was indicated by a feeling, or sense, that this group of ladies did not much seem to pay attention to much else due to a continual looking towards the darker cultured woman's direction. In this seemingly clutter of women, the darker cultured woman notices that the officer (within 15 minutes) of the last time he walked by seemed to be hanging around, out of sight, but you could just sense he was there. By this time, the darker cultured woman wondered what in the world was going on and thought within herself, maybe she should leave, but then quickly wondered why as she had not tried to do anything else but read her book!

Suddenly it seemed, as the darker cultured woman was still trying to read her book, she wondered why these women seemed to be giving her unasked for attention. Then this woman that seemed to have a position in the library literally turns from the huddled position with these young ladies and rises up straight (as if she lifted herself up very keenly, as if she were going to say something to the darker cultured woman who was still sitting quietly trying to read her book). The darker cultured woman begins to think to herself as she continued trying to read, *"is anyone else seeing this?"*

Well, the darker cultured woman kept her face glued to her book, and moments or minutes later, this lighter woman seemed to be able to gain her composure as she turned back to the ladies that still seemed to be hurdled close to her and they all turned and walked away. Soon after which, seemingly simultaneously, the officer (who did not seem far from the women) does another round as he passes the darker cultured woman.

Analysis

Well, some of you may think, so what. *This would be about right, my thoughts exactly, under normal circumstances*. However, it seems the police are showing up around any interactions having to do with lighter cultures who find themselves in awkward positions when the darker cultures come on the scene, *even when* the awkwardness seems to be coming solely (or initiated) from the lighter cultured communities (or personalities within the community).

I thought it best to bring up this particular example, to help bring to the forefront of what is continually happening among and around light and dark cultured interactions and/or events (or episodes), literally due to a *heightened sense* of ill-energetic spirit activity accumulating and growing among us as (already mentioned in this writing) and their attempt to **_pull both_** cultures continually into their (energetic spirit) realities, but for different reasons concerning us when, and as, they try to manifest (or reveal themselves in *ritual sytems they attempt to attach to us*, in hidden ways they become visual) among us. Why is this? Mt. 7.16-20. Mt 12.33.

The seemingly common thread in all of these scenarios and common theme throughout this book is that we are dealing, and/or should I say how we are (or are we) dealing, with this higher level of energetic spirit activity happening among us and to us. There are only 2 spiritual kingdom activities operating among us, only 2, no matter the religion or non-religious view(s). The Bible teaches us about the love of Christ and the ways of the Lord. The Lord also teaches us *not to fear* and gives us example of those who feared and of those who did not fear in the Bible. Rom. 14.17. Rev 16.10.

> "For God has not given us a spirit of fear but of power and of love and of a sound mind ..."
> 2Tim. 1.7. "There is no fear in love, but perfect love cast out fear, because fear hath torment ..."
> 1Jn 4.18  "Be careful for nothing but in every thing by prayer and supplication let your supplication with thanksgiving let requests be made known unto God ..." Phil 4.6-7. Rom 8.26. Rom 8.15.
> "So that we may boldly say, the Lord is my helper and I will not fear what man shall do unto me."
> Heb. 13.6.

In this scenario, this library woman seemed to be having what we can refer to as, energetic spirit manifestation(s) and she does not seem to have or express the ability to deal with how the energetic spirit is trying to operate in her life in this particular scene and so she keeps certain people around her, thinking this is helpful. If this were true, then why call and/or involve the police. **Where is the crime?** Jesus said my people perish for lack of knowledge. Hosea 4.6. First, I would like to tell this library woman, and those who find themselves in these types of energetic spirit episodes you, especially those in Christ or who claim Christ, and/or those trying to maintain their spirit lives in Christ, are not to lose their *life's focus* due to energetic spirit intrusions. We are to overcome them. *We are to resist them,* not make room for them, in Jesus name we are to stay on course in Christ and keep the faith. 2Tim 4.7. The Bible teaches us to submit to God, resist the devil (no matter what form he takes) and he will flee. James 4.7. However, in this case, it seemed this energetic spirit has so worked its spirit energy in this woman's life that now she apparently is following these spirit idols' leadings (yes these spirit energies become idols when you keep submitting to their leading, luring, and pullings of any ill-spirited energy). Corin. 12.2. God's Spirit energy operating through His people should express some consistent levels of His love over fear, His joy and peace over confusion. Jn. 4.13. Gal 5.22-25. Ps. 16.11. 2Tim 1.7. Corin. 13.11. Exo. 34.6. Jn 15.9014. See www.god.net.com. God's Spirit energy activity is not unsound, so this lets us know something is not quite right with this type of situation. This woman and those who find themselves in this type of energetic spirit activity are in need of **learning** how to resist, ill or dark energetic spirit activity. I pray this writing helps minister to you and where you may find yourself, is my prayer. In Christ we are commanded to submit to God and resist the devil (no matter what form or ideas he takes on) so the dark energetic spirit activity flees (in other words *how* is it going to flee if you don't resist it?) But in this case, this energetic spirit activity leads this woman to go before (evidently) this dark cultured woman. OK. Why? James 4.7. Biblically, it is revealed that:
Devil spirits (ill or negative energetic dark spirits) love drama. They like attention people, they have a passion to reveal and express their ill-spirited kingdom activity, and if they have to use you to do it, so be it, but you are not biblically supposed to submit to them, only to God's word and grace. Acts 19.11-20. Gal. 5. Rev. 16.10. James 4.7.

Why, because darkness represents a spiritual kingdom and they have their own agendas, people who don't realize this are usually pulled continually and continuously into dark spirit realms of activity and episodes of dark agendas along with the spiritual confusion and spiritual indifference they create by being on the scene, and by this literally pull you off course with God. Some people think they are safe if they do not claim a religion but not so. You either choose one or you are pulled off course with God or you are pulled and/or spirit forced into service by the dark agents among you as we see this could be potentially happening, or unfolding, in this scenario. So, we see again ignorance can be very dangerous. The energetic sin they eventually pull you into once they train you to obey them can become a very destructive pattern, not only to you and your family but can effect your generation as well, even your area of influence. This library woman probably needs help now, especially in how this negative energetic spirit activity is actually pulling her into the path of other cultures to do what … **cause drama, to express a dark energetic spirit system in operation before us!** This is another way darkness is revealing their influence in the Earth! Because they have no biblical authority, but evidently they can spiritually encroach with spirit energy all day long. Paul talked about people being led around by dumb idol (spirits). Corin. 12.2. Anyway this woman needs to learn how to resist the ill-spirit energy activity either by the ways already mentioned in this writing and/or by putting peppermint in water in a small water bottle or place peppermint on a napkin or tissue and place it on her body where you are having a manifestation (where one senses the energy is trying to manifest on the body) until it lifts please don't let the dark energy keep bubbling and/or vibrate within and/or outside. Upon the surface of your skin when you are at home, use the peppermint, to squelch it until it stops. There is always a purpose. They want to always vibrate upon your body – it helps create a place in your soul when they can stay attached to any part of your body. Why would you want to be pulled around all day long by dark energetic being activity, I have had to pull off the road because some people have just let the energy keep vibrating upon them, like it is so cute. But when they go anywhere, this growing mass of energy goes with them. I've detected this mass around certain drivers and I just pull off the road. It simply is not environmentally safe for others. This idea will also work for your phone, to help keep the lines clear, very important. Some people you call, if you have become sensitive in the spirit realm will just start having conversations on the phone, with the spirit energies stuck in the phone. _Please_ just get a new phone or use peppermint to wipe the phone as you are speaking, especially if people are manifesting spirit energy while you are speaking to them. It's not really them, it is the energy trying to get into their lives, as they are constantly looking for _places_ to manifest in humanity. Eph. 4.27. This does not necessarily mean that the energy will not come back but we are to subdue our ill-energetic spirit friends, causing the spiritual indifference among us, until the Lord reveals otherwise, however long it takes. That's the good fight of faith, we are still supposed to use our faith to please the only true and living God. 1Tim 6.12. In the time being, this will eventually break the negative energetic spirits activity concerning you on the scene. If she uses the spray she can just spray on her body wherever the energy tries to manifest. Even if the energy tries to pull you into a sleep or nap, just spray around yourself until it lifts and/or keep waving the napkin with the peppermint on it around your head until it lifts, if it is more convenient to do so. Sometimes just sitting on peppermint can prove helpful. These are only some suggestions that have worked, however you are able to pray and seek the Lord for other possible remedies. But _there is a need_ to hinder and/or stop what any negative ill-spirit energy is trying to do! But often, to stop it, you have to resist it, to get out of agreement with it naturally and spiritually so. James 4.7. The ladies who were with her as well, gathering together seemingly in fear, will **only breed a place for the negative energy spirit activity to operate** and grow because they seemed to be in a type of fear agreement and these beings feed off fear, hate, indifference, etc. I continually see a lot of this. We need to gather with flowcharts of faith to gain the ability to resist energetic spirit activity and at the same time it will help us to keep focused.

Jesus said, He did not give us the spirit of fear. Why are many trying to hold onto fear and resist the culture, (and then we want to bring our fear before others and just expect others to figure out what our problem is, really), especially if the fearful situation is coming from you? **Where is your faith?** Lk. 8.25.

Many want to call the police because they don't know how to deal with their strange energetic spirit activity trying to influence or lead them about. Amos 3.3. How is the policeman supposed to help regarding your spirit manifestation? How is the policeman supposed to:

Help you if your unrestrained spirit activity causes you to get up into someone's face, which causes you to be fearful, because you don't know what is going to happen?

If the police _you_ call don't seem to know deliverance or seem to have spiritual intelligence, how is he going to help you? Are the police you call supposed to help you hold onto or protect your excess spirit activity and fear? Then how do you find healing or release when the police come? What happens when the police you call needs just as much deliverance or release as you and he shows up with a gun? Some of the issues being realized in these scenarios are that it seems to be an ill-energetic spirit agenda to cause the lighter culture among us to manifest (causing them to become **spiritually indifferent**) with the person (darker culture you think is) causing you to have a negative reaction or literally feel offended, even when they have done nothing. The excess energetic spirit manifestation upon <u>your</u> body effecting <u>your</u> soul is causing <u>you</u> to feel spiritually indifferent, especially if or when <u>you</u> are <u>not rooted</u> in the word of God whenever any and/or most darker cultured people come into <u>your</u> environment. Mark 4.17. Meaning there is not enough word or knowledge of God's word to help you to resist negative ill-spirited energies when they rise within <u>your</u> soul and/ or upon <u>your</u> body. If the police you are dealing with do not understand excess spirit energy activity, how would that bring any sense of soundness or security, if the excess spirit energy now causes the police to manifest his hand that is on his gun. Do we not think it or should we consider how we could jeopardize others because we and/or someone we involve may need some level of spiritual release and/or need to learn how to resist certain levels of excess energetic spirit manifestation(s).

What looks like racial issues seem to be arising out of your own culture, due to your need as a culture, it seems on how to release and/or resist oneself from ill energetic spirit activity concerning you? Instead of thinking that when you have a manifestation, it must be somehow caused by darker cultures,it's <u>really playing out to be</u> a level of spiritual and biblical lack of knowledge of spiritual kingdom warring against the saints or those in Christ. Whether within your culture or between, darkness wants to break our bands of unity. Ps. 2.3. I wonder if you realize how much spiritual indifference and its influence among any one culture is being expressed towards another culture.

The rising episodes arising out of the manifesting spiritual indifference, being caused by excess spirit energy activity really begins to get your attention. It is your culture shushing your own culture, whenever anyone from the darker culture comes on the scene. As if there is some deep secret that no one can see but your culture, causing your spiritual indifference towards darker cultures, as if it were personal. No. This is the deception. It's the work of darkness that manifests or literally stirs your soul when a darker culture comes on the scene, even that rises or stirs your soul when it (the work of dark energetic spirit activity) rises against someone in your own culture when the person of your culture (usually a Christian) comes on the scene. There are only 2 spiritual kingdom operations operating among us. Only 2. So, whether in the home or business community, there seems to be continual evidence of negative spirit energies influencing you without resistance on your part, causing you to manifest as being spiritually indifferent towards the darker culture, to have issues with the darker culture. So then, an issue could be why is the lighter culture allowing for, literally making room (as a breeding place) for, this spiritual indifference?

Could we possibly realize, that my brother or sister must need some level of spiritual release from their spiritual indifferent towards another culture for any reason whenever they come on the scene. It is not always _safe_ to believe someone, anyone that seems to struggle often, in forgiving others or in giving grace to others. The point to those needing spiritual release from manifestations of spiritual indifference, _does not point to the opportunity of taking sides_ among you. If this is your view, then you also are in need of spiritual relase. And, I'm not being "deep." It is possible to learn how to resist the negative energetic spirits when they stir your soul. One way is by calling on the name of the Lord continually until it lifts. Another way is the Wash Flow Chart with the name of Jesus, a chart that _will better help you focus on the Lord_, instead of the trouble that the negative spirit energies are trying to engage you in. The word of the Lord has a greater force of energy if you will keep speaking on the name of Jesus until the dark ideologies or spirit energies stop engaging you. Often what I have seen is the unbelievers and/or satanist mixed in the majority among one saint. The one saint gets overcome because when the dark energies try to engage the saint, the unbeliever and/or Satanist rises up quickly because they realize quicker than you that Satan is trying to engage you in his work, which is usually trying to mock and/or ostracize. the saint in harassing ways until they leave but if you have a flow chart of scriptures, you'll be more prepared to resist the darkness that tries to engage you and/or their workers in your midst. You're better able to focus on Christ. Even invite Him into your midst as you begin to preoccupy yourself with speaking to yourself softly saying, Lord, I resist the energy in this place by the name of Jesus by the works of Christ and when you look up you'll see that the temptation is gone because Jesus is Lord, He has the greater energy. Many Christians and/or non-Christians do not realize the need to resist the energies (and/or presence) that accompany those with dark faith belief systems and how many get sucked into their dark realm (by the energetic spirit energy that accompanies them). No arguing just a silent resisting, by focusing on the energetic words of Christ. Isa. 26.3.

_Learning how to do this should be taught to everyone that has a soul and spirit life_ which can be effected by either spiritual kingdom activity concerning you, whether it is to offer you salvation and grace through Jesus Christ or whether a spiritual intrusion is coming as a darker spiritual kingdom activity to bring hurt, harm, or danger. Jn.10.10. No one culture corners the market on not needing some level of spiritual release and/or need to learn how to resist excessive dark spirit activity because negative spirit energies don't die. They are always trying to spiritually contaminate others and/or transform themselves until no longer recognized, but their spirit fruit is always dreadfully unfruitful (or unpleasant). Why listen to those spiritually contaminated among us. Give them a copy of this book and help us pray for one another. God has given us great Christian leaders such as:

> Joyce Meyer, James Dobson, Chuck Swindoll, Troy Brewer,
> Tommy Barnett, Jack Hayford, Charles Stanley, TD Jakes,
> Beth Moore, and others with Moody Broadcasting

to name a few. Yet, look at the power of culture to spiritually catch on to what is effecting or what is influencing (including spirit manifestations) cultures the most. This is their reality! What they are experiencing. More than what they are being told. This is why we need to learn how to dwell deep, so as to not be easily uprooted, in Jesus name. Therefore, we must learn how to deal with ill/negative energetic spirit manifestations and their ability to cause spiritual indifference, spiritual intolerance and perpetual spiritual hate. Spiritual indifference left unchecked turns quickly into spiritual intolerance, producing various fruits of division, strife, etc. as an expression of any level of spiritual indifference or hate as the fruit of spiritual intolerance. Eze. 25.15. Eze. 35.5.

It sort of threw me one day, not that I am perfect – but I allow Christ to perfect me, when I heard a Bible teacher's reply over the radio as a caller called in concerned about what darkness or Satan was doing in his life. But when the announcer didn't seem to have an answer he replied, I think we give Satan too much credit. I thought Mr. Radio teacher you still did not answer the question. Some might think you sounded more cynical than caring. Prov. 21.13. **Where** in the Bible does God say or indicate you give Satan too much credit, because someone is needing more understanding on how to resist what the enemy is doing? _God what kind of answer is that?_ This is how I learn, when I ask God questions. Sometimes we tell on ourselves, with replies like this, sometimes people are revealing that they too could have been spiritually effected themselves and so they cannot really respond in the best way. They can become unqualified to answer the question and also, being too spiritually effected, can make one seem to express the fruit of not really caring as Christ may intend. Mt. 12. I thought God, how is that a fair answer to someone with legitimate concerns? In light of this writing I would say that the caller had a real legitimate concern seeing that many among us are dying, being handicapped, and some are even going to churches with guns because of how darkness is operating in a person's soul. www.whitemankills9in charleston.scchurch.com. This caller's question was very legitimate because the men in the lighter culture, white men, are leading in suicide by 70%. So yes, there is a need to gain the ability to answer these types of questions and not brush them off lightly because someone is not qualified to answer. www.whatraceleadsinsuicide.com. www.northcarolina pastordisarmsgunman.com .

We can learn of those among us in need of any level of spiritual release (some call it healing) when our expressed fruit does not consistently line up with the kingdom we are claiming. This is why and how we can know when to pray for one another in Jesus name. James 5.16.

Mourn with those who mourn (or be concerned) … Rom 12.15. Ecc. 3.4.

_The Spiritual Root of the Matter is Found in Me_, helps one release and/or un-layer ourselves from less desirable, unfruitful spiritual energies, suicide included. We need to learn how to deal effectively when ill-energies try to effect us. Thank you Jesus!

Darkness can be a real taskmaster when it is trying to operate through a soul to hurt others or one self and make it seem like the person is doing it instead of pointing to the ability of ill-energetic spirits to take over a soul. Mt. 27.5. I thought, God where is the prophetic in the lighter cultures who you've trained just like you did me to help the people overcome when darkness is moving in our generation. Where are they? I only know of one and I listed her teaching and name in this writing. When darkness started attacking me with spiritual intrusions, I am glad God had compassion on me that He did not say, don't you think you are giving Satan too much credit? The Lord had compassion on my soul and led me through the darkness step by step giving me hope. God did not say shut up or get over it!

The Bible says weep with those who weep. In other words can we at least try to show some compassion or try to give someone hope and not cause others to wonder if you could be too spiritually effected to sympathize with those who are dealing with the pains that darkness can cause.

Joseph was subject to hard treatment, but the Lord was with him … Exo 3.7. Exo 1.11.

Our police are supposed to help protect the community. 2Corin. 4.4. Jn 1.5. Gal. 4.16. How are our policemen protecting the community if they are just as _spiritually effected_ as those in the community and/or seemingly have no greater spiritual intelligence than what the community seems to be suffering? Is it possible to help the community and divide it at the same time? How are the police to know when a person is being confronted with a spirit intrusion or if the spirit is actually coming through the person's soul, causing the spiritual indifference (also called a breach in the soul)? Gal. 5. How does anyone in the culture having a spirit intrusion that is causing the person in the culture to call the police, and the police come on the scene not knowing what to do if the spirit intrusion **begins to effect him** _(spirit energy can and does transfer), causing the officer to have a indifferent spirit transfer come upon him. Acts 19._

_How can the officer advise a person in the business community, if they have no spiritual intelligence?_ If these ideas are so, how can we continue to jeopardize our communities by calling police on the scene that do not have the spiritual intelligence nor faith to handle business communities that are dealing with spirit intrusions, manifesting as a spiritual type of disease (as indifference) spreading throughout community. If our officers do not realize that those dealing with spirit intrusions can and will manifest through people's personalities, personalities **that do not know how to release themselves** from ill-spirit personality activity causing the indifference. Especially if most of the business community are now on meds (trying to deal with their energetic spirit manifestations causing spiritual indifference whenever another culture comes on the scene), while trying to hold down a job. However, as we have seen with this library woman, taking meds does not necessarily stop the spirits energy from pulling and/or luring you into situations. It's why they can be seen as an energetic spirit activity. An activity, that can and should be understood and resisted. James 4.7. Why?

Dark energetic spirits are not sound. They are perverse and they will play out their perversion in and through whoever does not realize how to resist them.

Just like those who went to the church with guns (one was hesitant, one waited for the right time, indicating the level the energetic spirits were able effect or breach their souls to operate in their lives).

… James 4.7, James 1.14-15, Jude 1.4, 2Corin. 5.10, Corin. 6.9.

Mr. Officer, if energetic alien spirit beings (and the ways they operate as listed in this book) can create an "area 51" in our army community, how is it you don't think they can get into one culture and dominate it against another culture. Even cause one culture to rise against another by using or crying **"fear or race"** as an energetic spirit tactic. Then you think that if you show up with your gun in our communities, you'll help one culture not to be fearful about another culture because you come on the scene. Really. _Would you be putting yourself in the place of God and not get God's attention_ Exo. 2.3. Well, what do you think it looks like? Innocent people are dying, sure it may not be your intent, but ill-energetic spirits have their own agenda and they do not necessarily care who they can cause to help them reach their dark spirit kingdom agenda. They did **not** stop with NASA! We need quality policing, based on intelligence (spiritual intelligence) in whatever area is needed, more than quantity policing with the ability to seek out the intelligence when needed to make the community and its habitants **safer**. Our communities are not necessarily more safe if you show up with no intelligence that is needed for you to help the whole community to be safer, not the limited intelligence that supports dividing community and causing community to strive instead of find a common peace. Whether it is something you can see or not see, the Bible says you know them by their fruit! Mt.12. If you say, I don't know the Bible, then your intelligence is limited in the area that is needed to help community because you need to understand the things that can and do, effect _all_ of the community that you are required to keep safe, if not you are too limited to do your job. To whom much is given, much will be required. Lk 12.48.

If the majority of the business community are calling you because they are afraid of this or that, saying please come, please come, etc., Since we are dealing with an excess of energetic spirit activity in the business as well as personal communities, "_is it a "stretch"_ to consider that the business community needs to learn how to more effectively deal with excess spirit activity to the degree they think they may need police protection. Mr. Officer, can we realize that this similar type of excess spirit activity manifested generations ago during Martin Luther King's times? The Bible says there is nothing new under the sun.

## _It wasn't a racial issue then and it isn't a racial issue now!_

Its spiritual – always was, always will be. There is nothing new under the sun. Ecc. 1.9.
Come on! If the alien spirit beings were so successful in crying "race, race" **why not** do it again to help them accomplish their spirit operation's kingdom agenda to divide and destroy. Jn. 1010. Rev.16.

How many times does the black culture or whatever cultures these energetic beings want to attack whenever they visit earth, have to deal with negative spirit (energy) activity coming through those with little to no spiritual intelligence? They say our communities, our nation _is as strong as our weakest link_.
Would you be helping us find our weakest biblical link and/or another level of intelligence among us?

The weakest link is the area or place where darkness or destruction etc., is able to get through, spiritually or naturally so. So who's side are you on? Who is on the Lord's side? Exo. 32.26.

We need everyone to gain in spiritual intelligence, please! We cannot trust in our own abilities alone, we need spiritual intelligence when dealing with ill-spirit intelligence. Prov. 28.26.All judgment comes from the Lord! **Who** hath ears to hear? Mt 13.9. Lord, help us to educate those who **need** spiritual intelligence. Ignorance is not working for us, it seems to cause division as well as being an energetic spirit tool for spiritual indifference.

The Bible contains spiritual intelligence. The Bible contains history. Without it people are perishing! Hosea 4.1. Hosea 4.6. Eph. 4.16.
Jn. 15.21. This is not about religion, it is about spiritual intelligence! Job 21.14.Rom 1.28. We need spiritual intelligence. When hell comes against any of us, we don't necessarily need humanity with limited spiritual intelligence, seemingly *siding with darkness* because they have no spiritual intelligence (or spiritual maturity). **Some think** that every energetic spirit energy that moves you is to be listened to. WHO TOLD YOU THAT? Not God. God does not operate against Himself.

> God is not sharing His glory with low level energetic alien beings. Why would He?
> ***He is God!***   Isa 42.8

God is Spirit. God is good. Who are you listening to? *We can tell by what you do*. Prov. 23.7.There are only 2 spiritual kingdoms operating among us only 2. Both are influencing mankind. Ask the psychiatrist and psychologist. They say history repeats itself. Does this mean that if ignorance is a part of our history, it *has* to repeat itself also

> How is it that our police would be available to be used as a force again whenever we have an excess of dark spirit activity wanting to rise up against darker cultures and/or cultures of their choice, especially in traffic situations. There was Rosa Parks in 1955 along with Sandra Bland among others in 2015 and still happening today!

I am not saying that our police should major in ministry, as well as policing, but that they should <u>gain</u> enough spiritual intelligence to be part of the solution among us, not always a part of the problem due to consistent spiritual and biblical ignorance among us.

We need spiritual intelligence from the pulpit to the pew. In the business community to the presidency! We all need to <u>grow up spiritually</u>. *We all need salvation!* Rom. 1.16. Eph. 2.8-9. Rom 10.9-10. Acts 4.12.

<u>Only</u> God offers salvation in the earth. God is not necessarily every spirit acting out in your life, so <u>learn</u> how to resist the negative energy spirit activity. We can all sleep better at night, knowing that more among us are better able to preserve their lives and families by gaining a knowledge of spiritual intelligence that is able to help us stay on our life's course. Ps.89.6. Ps. 113.5. Isa 46.5.Isa 40.25. Rom. 10.13.
It is the spirit of domination behind the energetic energies operating through division and spiritual indifference. What is interesting is when the spirit of domination is trying to operate energetically within any one culture it can have the same effect. If the darker culture is working alongside a lighter cultured person, who may have a spiritual manifestation of indifference and calls the police, sooner or later this energy has the ability to transfer over to the darker culture that works along the lighter cultured person that has the manifestation. What would this look like?

> Potentially, say the darker cultured person just referenced above also works at Big Restaurant, for example, as a manager. While working, say a certain darker cultured person comes in that happens to be a Christian. This could irritate any negative spirit energies in any environment they are claiming, They would then manifest on the darker cultured manager in this restaurant who has been already spiritually processed and/affected who would then become spiritually indifferent just by looking at a saint in Christ. They would then call the police with an illogical concern, not realizing their feelings of indifference are coming from a spirit trying to operate in the soul. Then the police would drive up to circle around the

restaurant and seem to linger around the person, who happens to be Christian, because the negative energies operating upon the police in this spiritually effected territory can discern those of light.

If the spirit of domination is working in a family of any culture, a spirit of indifference could rise up like Cain against Able. Gen 4. This is why it is necessary to set up boundaries of behavior to <u>not</u> give place to darkness, whenever and whomever it would work through. Usually truth works but those with little faith may look towards civil laws to protect. Now the issue is that our laws of the land of protection are being broken down and literally ignored by those being effected by negative energies, trying to rule through men (and their positions) among us. Men that need to learn how to release themselves from that which is trying to overcome their souls in order to rule through them.

This is also to say that when there is consistent ignoring of the excess spiritual energies in one's life, culture, church and city, etc., the negative spirit energy of domination will continue to develop. First surfaces the spiritual indifference, then the uncontrollable hate will grow, (Bible calls it perpetual hate). Because these beings are emotional, they will then think their hate feeling is reason enough and becomes their right or platform by which to continue eroding the life (or lives) they are trying to come against (or take). The DNA, found in John 10.10; never changes – they come to kill, still and destroy. These beings do not try to change men, nor negotiate. They simply release enough of their negative spirit DNA to become the men they desire to work through. This is a powerful dark spirit kingdom strategy, and it is how they are able to continue their secret (but visual) work among us. They realize most have not learned to resist them, can potentially become them, or what is referred to as too spiritually effected. And what does this look like?

Well, I can say I am not as concerned with other nations trying to destroy us. I would be more concerned about the operation of darkness in our midst, destroying men (by becoming men, or forming or fitting themselves within man's physical structure) from the inside out, by what is clearly ignorance on our part if we allow these beings to do so. Why there isn't a spiritual state of alarm sounding as a trumpet in our nation is beyond me. Let's look at these energetic spirit beings' activity among us a bit closer (and please bear with me), I just feel the Lord wants me to tell you what I have been witnessing and seeing.

Listen, I have seen, more than once (plus I have been told by another seeing this same incident) at our rest areas, where a Christian is taking a leisure walk (where people are free to walk their dogs at one end of the rest area). Suddenly, a line of truck drivers all get out of their trucks <u>at the same time</u>, walk towards the hood of their trucks, and look towards the Christian. Perhaps that these energies have been hounding to use or spiritually effect, a type of simultaneous dark spirit energetic allegiance to let this Christian know and realize their energetic spirit influence over men in areas of industry. Their ill-energetic spirit ability works in the lives and souls of our truck drivers to collectively command their allegiance at will! 2Tim. 2.26. I call this a type of demonic synchronizing.

Then to hear of about 62 police chasing down one car with 2 people in it. Once these 2 people were surrounded, an officer jumps on the hood of the car and unloads bullets into the vehicle and the people inside the car had no guns! www.clevelandofficeracquittedinkillingunarmedcoupleincar.com. Another type of demonic synchronizing! There are only 2 spiritual kingdom operations going on and happening among us, only 2! The correct God does not bring confusion to the table, so confusion in any incident should raise a red flag in one's soul. Corin. 14.33.

Why and how are people allowing themselves to be led by idol spirit activity and operations against one another? Could it be due to not realizing the need to resist any spirit energy that comes ritually upon men to train them to obey? Why would our officers learn to obey energetic spirit beings more than our natural civil laws when dealing with the community? Probably because energetic spirit beings don't seem to let up. Well, who is training our officers not to obey their intrusive energy activities listed in this writing? So why can't we just learn to teach why they are manifesting and how to resist them? If the beings are operating for the last 50+ years and they continue to be the cause of high mental statistics (suicide and physical ailments among us), why can't we just learn some biblical intelligence, enough to help us resist their perverted and demented influences? Can we just get over the fascination that, though they like to operate invisibly, they are **clearly seen** among us by the troubles they create in trying to merge into a society that does not belong to them? Ps. 115.16.

So, I did not find it unusual to hear that two of our navy went off-course 15 miles in international water due to a nagivational error – only to find themselves in Iranian territory! Are you kidding me! Please hear me. **This is the level** of energetic spirit kingdom activity and influence of those in key positions among us. There is research that reveals whole U.S. ships have been missing. There is research to show that people have not only been missing but had interaction with alien spirit energies before their disappearance. Lord, help us to see that just like the collective truck drivers and dark police synchronizing incidences, in the examples above, _again is  uncovering the alien spirit kingdom's influence among us_ **when there is no resistance**. James 4.7. This has been a day to day spirit intrusion among men, growing over 50 years now. Is it because we, as a family, community, business, and market place of society have been too collectively spiritually effected? Lord Jesus, please help us to see that with You we can do all things through Christ who strengthens us. _Open our eyes to see that we have a part to play here_, that we can learn how to resist their influence instead of allowing them to operate through us to divide us, make us sick, take our jobs and literally cause those in dark spirit systems to take over. Causing believers to work for them and then kill us, mostly with the white culture leading in 70% of suicides among us. Let me park here for a minute!

Satan workers among us are working in allegiance with the energetic beings to force Christians in the market places to work by their dark spirit initiatives to force out of jobs whom their energetic spirit beings are pointing out. People are losing their jobs for dumb reasons. Dumb idols. Dumb reasons. So it is the majority of the white culture causing this and in this manner are training people to obey their spirit energies. In this way the people learn to pick up on the white cultures effected by negative spirit energies when they come to manifest. People are being forced on their jobs to huddle when they get a break or when they are being summoned by spirit energies ruling usually those in the lighter cultures on their jobs, so the energies can manifest collectively upon them! And 70% of the white culture are committing suicide. So how faithful are these beings to whom they use to exploit our culture, our jobs, and our families?

I have seen blacks walk off their job because they did not want to be a part of these types of dark energetic spirit ritual huddles going on among us. So many jobs have become the new congregations. So this is where we need ministry pastors.

When these types are not even culture groups they become demonic or dark spirited groups because they allow these beings (ill-energetic beings) to work through the people to bear rule at the work place. All because people are afraid to resist these beings which may mean losing their jobs. All because dark spirited influences are working to encourage people to fit in and obey what darkness is doing among them. Those with dark souls will encourage dark spirited allegiance. Sometimes they watch if the people obey the dark spirit energies operating there, if not the ones with the dark soul will start causing trouble for the Christians. Other cultures being persecuted for their faith are needing safe places in the community to survive. We need to find jobs that are safe places among us. Not jobs that teach you how to obey dark spirit idols. We need to understand the depths of the dark deprivation happening among us.

We do not realize that many more women used to drive with their men in the big rigs. However, these dark ill-spirited energies began "fighting, the women on the trucks with penetrating spirit energies" until they could not take it. Some have been really hurt, physically, while the men stand by as idle watchers, dumb founded as to what to do. If women were seen at some trucking industries, those with dark spirit souls would gather the other workers together for collective energy power, and then release these cumulative energies to any woman they wanted off the property. The energies would literally get or work themselves into the woman's body and cause her to act out as strange, or even cause her to come up to certain men or pull down her pants and the demonic beat and demonic synchronizing goes on. Why we do not have laws on the book for those who engage others to cause civil problems is beyond me. This is where ministry is needed, pastors. Then people that leave spiritually hostile trucking companies take this negative spirit energy activity with them and then the spirit will reproduce itself or manifest as it has on a person's new job. So, if people in trucking companies were forced to resist those of light energies in Christ and say start a new job at a rest area, then whenever a darker cultured person and/or one with Christ spirit energy comes on the scene, the energy gets offended through the rest area worker and calls the police to come and make this person leave the rest area. Even though the person, seeming to bother the rest area person, has committed no crime. These are continued reasons why and how our communities are becoming (and have become) territorial among us. Those energetic beings have effected and needed spiritual release from these beings, who have decided they want our families, friendships, jobs, communities and our nation. This is how these perverted beings are pressuring Christians on their jobs and communities, by those needing release and those who need to gain the ability to resist these beings. Just imagine if enough of us resisted them, they may leave! But first Pastor, people need to learn how to get over the fear of them and those they work with that help cause them to fear them. I have never seen so much fear, territories of fear. All because we are not teaching the people what Jesus said, to submit to God, resist them and they will flee. James 4.7. The book: The Spiritual Root of the Matter is Found in Me speaks to those needing to learn how. So where's the "faith in Christ" territories? This is where I want to be found when Jesus returns! Amen. Phil. 4.13.

Lord, please help us save our nation. Help us minister where the people are at so we can stop backing up our society, like a clogged toilet with the excess spirit energies. We repent. www.2navyshipsoffcourse.com.

Could we discern, in this example, who would need spiritual release and/or who would need to learn how to resist negative energetic spirit activity in their environment(s)? Weren't Sodom and Gomorrah destroyed because they lost their ability to discern evil? You need to know and realize truth in order to discern evil.

***Let's pray,***

Lord, we come repenting before you. We come praying and repenting for all cultures, business, marketplace, community sins, and sins of our nation. We pray for all the needs to be met including any healing needs of the mind, body, soul, spirit life and relationships in Jesus name. When one suffers, Lord, we all suffer. Corin. 12.26. James 5.16. Heal us from being used by dark spirit energetic intentions to:

- destroy one another's faith or good intentions within our own cultures nor among other cultures in Jesus name.

- to not side with, nor be led into the whoredom within our cultures, nor the cultures of others, for whoredom is the mistress witchcraft. Help us be strong enough in our faith to resist this type of dark allegiance. James 4.7

- Help us not be deceived in these areas by those spiritually effected who say they are our friends, family nor those in positions at our job. Help us be strong in faith to not fear those who have been spiritually infected, whose job in darkness is to spiritually effect others and/or act indifferent or intolerant of others.

- Help us learn to direct those spiritually effected and/or ignorant of spiritual things to safe places to get help. Help us to be safe places for each other. Help us to spiritually and naturally protect and prefer one another; that we can learn to be safe places for each other. Teach us how to protect, prefer our family again. Help us to cultivate safe environments at home, work and community with spiritual intelligence.

Lord, remove the spiritual blinders among us so we can see and give us wisdom to know and realize what needs to be done, to pull and lift ourselves out of this darkness in Jesus name. Lord, You have given the Earth to men. Help us to keep the Earth and blessing of the Earth, in Jesus name. Lord, we are repenting as a nation! Lord, help us to do better and be better, more responsible with the Bible knowledge You have given us. Lord, give us the *spiritual intelligence needed* to overcome our enemies in Jesus name!

Lord, protect us from the enemy intentions that You are revealing to us, even in this writing, in Jesus name. Lord, let not the enemies operating among us cause our land to become void, defiled, nor perverse through men as in the days of Genesis. Lord, save us again so that we can celebrate You in our midst again. Lord, how can we give our children hope for tomorrow? Our hope is in You, Lord. Give us counsel. Give us help. Give us hope. Roman 15.13. Be our voice among the nations. Be the God, the only God of our nation! Help us to avoid and even flee from dark ignorant counsel among us. We need truth. Lord, Your truth sustains. Remove the dark clouds (the things going on behind the scenes) so we can see that we are surrounded by so great a cloud of witnesses. Heb 12.2.

Help us to see that it does not matter how big the wall (the troubles or issues we face) if we don't man the gates of our soul, the gate between our ears. That our mind thinking, knowledge or lack of, is also between the ear gates. Help us fill our gates with truth, the truth that makes us more than conquerors. The truth that sets us free. Jn. 8.32.The truth that keeps us free. Help us to reprioritize our lives to man our gates with Your truth, to seek first the kingdom of God and Your righteousness. Give us the spiritual intelligence to know and understand that Your biblical and spiritual principles work. Lord, help us to not miss You, in this season of our lives. *Help us to not miss You among us and* Your desire to help us. We need Your truth even to realize this for You are the only God that offers salvation, in the heavens and in the earth. In Jesus name we pray for one another that we may be healed. Lord, we pray save our nation for Your name sake alone for we are the children of the prophets – Abraham, Issac and Jacob. In Jesus name, hear our cry among the nations. Lord, we can't imagine life without You! Lord, lead us in Your truth and teach us again, for you are the God of our salvation. Ps 5.5. Lord, You are still the way, the truth, and the life. Jn 14.6. Rom. 10.9. Lord, help us silence the things among us that continue to exalt itself against the knowledge of God for we see that ignorance of You is not helping us. 2Corin 10.5. James 5.16. 1Tim. 2.1. Eph. 6.18. Phil. 4.6.Thess 5.25. Col.4.2. We pray that Your word have free course once again in our nation. 2Thess.3.1. Lord, we loose the sword of truth in our land, to pull down every stronghold that tries to resist truth in Jesus name. 2Cor. 10.4.Mt. 6.33. Col. 2.8. Lord, we are seeking Your grace within and among our cultures. Titus 2.11.We pray this prayer will not return void but accomplish what You will, for Your glory. In Jesus name, we thank You for all things. Lord, help us to reconcile. Lord, reconcile our cultures and make us stronger and one in Christ! Those with understanding if the Spirit of the Lord is witnessing and stirring your souls, please continue praying and pray for me also, in Jesus name! Thank you! And everybody said Amen.

Example 4

The present Missouri situation, especially since it is not far from the Ferguson situation, continues to set the tone for what seems to be historical racial concerns. The Missouri Tigers are to be commended, along with other students taking their stand, for the seemingly growing display of those (which is everyone) in need of racial and spiritual release and healing on many various levels.

However, I believe there is a deeper level that no one is addressing and that I have been speaking of in this writing. Seemingly, no one is connecting the growing effects of the spiritual alien energetic influences happening among us that were initially invited by NASA research. Especially when the growing racial tensions are clearly energetic alien spirited agendas. So in this respect we are not really addressing the root of these issues and growing community concerns. We only seem to keep putting out the wild fires they create.

It is as NASA has always done to keep its spiritual alien spirit research interactions (and their energetic invasion) private. Research reveals that NASA could not keep their alien spirit research confidential. This continues to lead to ongoing secret spiritual alien energetic activities among us in the business and private sector – and their abilities to secretly cause many of our mainline police catastrophes of festering and excelling racial tensions. The spiritual alien intrusion are revealing their ongoing efforts to cause and create disharmonious relations, not only in the workplace, but in the marketplace on many personal levels. On many levels that are not really openly expressed but their spiritual alien intentions just keep seeming to manifest among us privately, as well as in the news, such as:

> How energetic alien influences are found trying to interact when we deal with anyone in community. Even a simple ill spirit unction in one's soul can manifest in a person's body (as pain) as a signal and a sign to not do business as usual with certain cultures that come by. These are spiritual indifferences are being created by energetic spirit realities operating among us.

All because people are and have become too spiritually effected by the spiritual alien intrusion agenda, like NASA, and now can be considered part of the issue. So in this respect, if what is and/or continues to be happening to Missouri historically can be considered an energetic spiritual alien intrusion, then those in leadership positions over different cultured groups are not able nor at liberty to straighten out any racial disturbance because they have apparently been too spiritually energetically effected in their soul and body. This, and such like incidences continuing to play out is what we are really dealing with in our culture and our communities – the energetic spiritual alien agenda. We have seemingly tried to keep spiritual contamination out of our society but in light of all the information in this writing, it is no longer possible.

Example 5

Susan, wife of the late Robin Williams, spoke recently for the first time regarding her husband in the November 16, 2015 issue of **People Magazine**.

Susan tells us of some of the many symptoms that her husband was actually dealing with. In light of this reading, it seemed appropriate to list some of the symptoms and experiences that Robin was dealing with, much of which can be found in this writing, that points to an energetic spirit activity happening here also such as:

- a variety of unusual symptoms

- heightened levels of anxiety, delusions and restricted movements

- a pain in his gut

- elevated cortisol levels and sleeplessness

- intermittent symptoms, could come on acutely. However, further study on intermittent and/or acute symptoms could also include severe verbal outbursts, irritable, impulsive, aggressive (even hostile) can come into play. Intermittent symptoms can be considered an explosive disorder and/or an impulse control disorder known or realized by sudden episodes of unwanted anger.

Susan would also begin to notice other symptoms such as:

- trembling in Robin's left hand (consistently)

- minor delusions, repeated fears

- a lack of clarity

Some doctors said Williams suffered from DLB or Dementia with Lewy Bodies, which can cause changes, fluctuating in his mind (or mental status) along with:

- hallucinations

- and impaired motor functions (this diagnosis could only come after an autopsy)

Another doctor would say he suffered from Parkinson's disease. Here Robin would be prescribed a wide range of treatments. Yet, the continued troubles of his mental symptoms continued to increase.

Robin would begin to ask doctors if he could be suffering also from Alzheimer and/or schizophrenia.

Robin would also suffer from:

- severe anxiety attacks that sometimes seemed to be caused or initiated by certain people looking at him
- a growing loss of control
- off-balanced
- and sometimes trance-like states

I could only imagine Susan feeling helpless, perhaps still trying to wrap her head around that this was actually happening. As she said in the article that she felt that her husband was literally disintegrating before her eyes. However, what I think that she did not say as well as others on this topic, is that one symptom that seems to be common with the symptoms is a pattern or type of systematic heat that seems to come before and/or during any of the symptoms. It is how I learned to realize that an energetic intrusion was taking place and I knew I had to resist the heat that seemed to bring on the symptoms. This is key!

After Robin's death, an autopsy revealed that every tissue in Robin's brain was ravished! Please, hear my heart! Someone needs to know, realize and understand that from my own experiences, some of which are evidenced by pictures in this writing reveal energetic spirit activity. Which causes me to believe that Robin also was dealing with a very vivid description of energetic alien-spirit assignment (or other worldly being that evidently attached to Robin's life and soul).

These beings work on many levels, including the ability to cause a person to disintegrate from within. These types of energetic beings can attack and/or attach within or without the body by first removing a person's energy field and/or spiritually effect it enough where anyone or anything could get to this person.

Paul spoke of warring within and without the body ...

Some worldly beings can work or operate independently of other beings. Some of these beings could and do attach for more fleshly, carnal reasons such as jealousy or even idolatry. Some look at idolatry as having something that may be placed at a higher value than ones relationship with the Lord. But now there is a need to consider that worldly beings working energetically among us are and can be found having attached to their subject to the degree that they are the ones forcing a person into idolatry! When there is no resistance. Gal. 5. This, therefore, is another form of idolatry that one must also learn how to resist.

Example 6

Here we have person who walks into a store called "B" to look for certain equipment. As the person walks in the store, they are greeted at the door and asked what is it they can be helped with. The person tells the greeter at the door, who then sends the person toward the back of the store to ask a certain employee who works in the area about the item that the person is interested in.

The person begins to engage the worker, who asks politely how they can help. OK. The person begins to tell what they are looking for and the worker says that they do not have the item in the store but that it can be ordered. However, the conversation then begins to take a turn after the worker begins to talk about what they are about to graduate from. Well, the customer congratulates the worker, then the customer begins to speak about their other interests. Before you know it, the worker is getting restless and begins to look so but the conversation is still interesting to the customer. As the customer continues to talk, talk, talk and the worker stands up and his hand reaches to press a button. Then the worker seems to back up slowly, as other men begin to approach their situation, causing the customer to begin to feel uncomfortable. Well by the time the other workers get closer and closer the customer says to the worker, it was great meeting with you and, again, congratulations on your graduation!

This scene started innocent enough and began with common type communication, however by the worker getting uncomfortable, signaled by his pressing a button, backing up as other workers came to the scene or should I say to the rescue. Well, you can interpret this any way you chose but this is what happened.

Because of the fact that many among us now have been going through various types of spiritual processing some can spiritually discern, others are yet learning.

Question: was the customer a problem customer and does this often happen to this customer and/or to this business?

No, this does not always happen to this customer however, if it did occur, it seemed to happen under certain situations. When certain energetic spirit beings are trying to attach and/or control a person's life, it seems these beings are always trying to get their attention. If energetic beings can't and/or are not getting the attention they want, they will literally manifest in the environment to restrain whomever they can, by those who have already been energetically effected in the environment in these types of situations. But more so we note that the business environment has become spiritually processed to then operate on a higher dimensional realm, during the course of regular business.

Therefore, this was not a situation where the customer wanted to be annoying but both were being spiritually pulled on to literally engage the customer endlessly, not because the customer wanted to but because energetic beings were literally causing the annoyance themselves. Perhaps, because they were annoyed with the person not willing participate with what these energetic beings activity. The customer should <u>not</u> be looked at indifferently and/or as if he (or she) was are the issue. It is the customer's environment being intruded upon with the help of the worker's spiritual environment.

All that was needed was for the worker to get up and turn away from the customer and begin to walk away; this perhaps would have broken the energetic grip on the customer. Also:

> Either the customer and/or the employee, whichever was not being spiritually gripped, could have a spray bottle with water (sprayed either between the two to break the grip and/or above the head). What is happening among us is not always about us!

No drama was needed. We have been forced as a society, community, family, etc., to live among these energetic beings. Therefore, we may need each other's help but **the help we need as a community, family and society will not come without an understanding of what these energetic beings are doing here** *because they are trying to pull us into their reality*. And then learn to recognize those who among us are effected too. Realize that energetic beings have caused some of us to be <u>*unsafe places for others*</u>, due to their intrusion, until others understand the need to learn how to effectively resist these beings. James 4.7. There are groups of people, spiritually effected, engaged in various spirit rejected activities towards humanity. These energetic alien spirit beings are, forging their way through, not only our society, but seemingly all societies! Even Christians can be found engaging in this type of energetic spirit activity, not necessarily because they want to, but because they are continually being too spiritually effected by these beings in the privacy of their own homes. Who else is teaching how to resist these beings enough to hold on to your own soul and right mind? Sometimes, we need to just come out from among them. 2Corin. 6.17.

# Flee idolatry!
Corin. 10.14

These energetic spirit beings can and will attack ritually and/or religiously (whether a person is religious or not). Please hear me, these beings have something they want from us in order to express themselves in our world and that is a "body"! Jude 9. However, long it takes, these energetic beings seem content with the subjects they chose. The concern is that those humans, whom they force into their energetic reality, usually become a menace to our jobs, community and society. Because their subjects, then, usually take on the energetic spirit's agenda and initiatives _to control in the territory they are in_ which usually encroaches on someone else's civil rights. This leads me to:

Example 7

A customer (should it matter if this customer appeared to be of a different culture) goes to _Hotel Issues_, for one night. After falling asleep, suddenly the customer is awakened by what seems like a sudden burst of excess spirit energy matter* coming from someone in the next room by what seems like an energy jolt upon certain private areas of the body. So the customer arises, still tired, looking at the clock notes that he or she had only been sleeping for maybe an hour or so. So the customer gets up, gets dressed. You could say _forced out of the hotel room by this uninvited excess of energy spirit activity_ that had to have come from a source effected by it a person evidently with energy issues – Ecc. 3.1. Spiritual energy activity can effect the physical body (Job 4.15) and drives to the nearest rest area to try to get a good nights sleep because of the rest that is needed in order to be able to go to work and/or function in the morning. _Was this fair_? Paying for a full night of rest but only able to get 1 hour of rest in the hotel (because of someone who is apparently effecting others at the hotel), and then leaving the hotel to find rest elsewhere, probably at an available rest area due to the _silent noise_ at the hotel environment.

---

*all matter (even spirit matter) takes up space, whether visible or not (www.allmattertakesupspace.com).

Another customer goes to _Hotel Rough_ and pays for a couple nights. As the customer is taking in some of their personal things, certain people seem to be walking by laughing out loud, seemingly with no cares of the verbal noise of the laughter they are making. As the customer prepares for bed later that night, suddenly, the customer senses a burst of spiritual energy matter coming upon him or her from the direction of upstairs. When this strange unrestful spirit energy matter does not let up, the customer decides to leave. As they leave, they can hear the shower come on upstairs _as well as_ furniture being pushed around. The customer then goes back to the hotel registration desk and asks "Did the hotel put someone upstairs over them?" The hotel personnel promptly says no. The customer was too tired to ask the clerk, if not, then who was using the shower upstairs? The customer then cancels his or her room. The customer could argue that there was someone upstairs because they heard the shower going as well as furniture being moved. But what is the use – it just didn't seem fair! What if a current or previous employee (Somehow still had access to a type of universal key) is trying to operate behind the scenes and the clerk simply did not know it? The customer then goes to the first rest area they see to try to get some sleep, so that they are able to work or function in the morning. _Did this seem fair?_

Another customer goes to _Hotel Deceit_, (does it matter that the customer is of a different culture) gets a room for one night. Some clerks needing spiritual release will place certain darker cultures in rooms for their behind the scenes "spooky activity." <u>This</u> time the customer only eats and takes a shower, then leaves when night comes due to those people with excess energy activity concerns (who can't find help) – and becomes an unsafe place for others to be around, because some excessive spirit energies actually have the ability to leave the person they have attached to, then attack others into an unrest state until they leave the area (because these beings are territorial), will try to pull you into their reality). Due to previous hotel experiences, _the customer is now concerned due to how excess spirit energetic beings are operating in many, many hotels_ by new guests that come to the hotel's facility. So the customer goes to the rest area, sleeps and then goes back to hotel Deceit around 8 or 9 am, to perhaps wash up and get to work. The customer figures their check out time is noon and the customer still had their key and it should not be a problem. **However**, the customer noted that someone had cleaned their room. OK but what happened to the customer's right to the room until noon. What if the customer needed to come back to the rest area before noon to catch a few hours of sleep, perhaps due to being awakened by a certain police officers activity? Does cleaning the room before the rooms scheduled time availability automatically cancel what the customer paid for? As the customer began to leave the building, he or she noted that a policeman had begun driving by (almost simultaneously). As the customer began to get into he or she's car, it was noted that a truck that was parked by the exit door (where the customer come out of). Someone was in the vehicle seemingly preoccupied with observing them. As the customer began to pull out, they noted that this mysterious truck parked by the exit door also began to leave along with the customer. The customer also noted that this person seemed to drive close to their vehicle's bumper and turn in the same direction and stop at the same traffic light

(I have actually viewed an officer do this to a person at a rest area). At this light the customer turned left and the mysterious truck at the hotel turned right. Did the customer do something to warrant this unnecessary silly attention or was this normal hotel activity?

Please bear with me. This may seem like tedious information, however, if the hotel's questionable activities are happening in conjunction with those being *spiritually effected* by alien energetic spirit matter activity (that can be observed); then the people will take on any alienist activity in that territory which is working against any cultural unity, and the bizarre activity is being enforced by police as they are called to the scene? This is unless the people in these hotel environments have gained the ability to resist negative spirit energy matter activity. *Where is the justice*? Is there no justice for those who are being forced to pay for services they are _not_ getting due to spiritual ignorance and/or the non-caring stance for the well-being of another to get rest and/or sleep. Is hotel management out of touch with the customers needs and well-being or are they also too spiritually energetically effected?

There is a lot more than meets the eye with these hotel scenarios. Such as the alien spirit energy activity that may attach to some family members in a community which may cause unrest within the family? Often times, families will send a member (or leave themselves) with unrestful or even violent type energy personalities to hotels so the family can sleep (because energetic spirit beings are territorial and will effect those they can in the environment they have attached to). Acts 19.16. The same thing happens to _others_ trying to find rest in the community or inter-state hotels, who are apparently rudely awakened by what is already energetically happening in the hotel environment to the customer's surprise. So, these customers seeking rest are awakened, get up in the middle of the night and go to the rest areas.

> What other refuge (sleep refuge) is available in our communities?
> For those who need intruding spiritual releases, just so they can
> get rest or sleep?

I often wondered if hotels even thought of spraying their beds with some type of effective Lysol Disinfectant spray, even out of consideration, with these types of energetic spirit realities happening in our hotels collectively. These are not isolated events or activities, people. Once I sprayed a bed down with Lysol and a few minutes later someone sat on the bed and said something had flown out of the mattress! Some hotels seem to get really upset if you spray with anything. I think this would be the hotels that one may not want to return to. I'm just sayin'!

Is it a far stretch to realize that some guests have dark spirited professions, or just have dark spirited personalities who visit hotels and sometimes their excess energies will choose to stay in certain mattresses, closets, bathrooms (after all this is a free country). I think? Some with dark personalities are spiritually skilled enough to spot those in Christ with the light, and it will upset the darkness operating in and through them. You can literally watch them get their spirit attitude on, watch room you go to. Then zap until you leave the hotel. Come on, what else are they going to do for "sport!" Some are so spiritually ill-effected they don't even realize it. This is when they will literally speak out for dark rights and then help work to take away your _____! Different levels of spiritual healing and greater understanding of how those effected need some level of spiritual release so as to not make it their life's endeavor to live to effect other families, communities, environments and societies. The only Being that can fix us is **God Himself!** Because no matter the spiritual interests among us, there are only 2 spiritual kingdom activities operating among us. Only 2!

Then we find another twist to these types of hotel issues, or concerns, or unsettling events regarding people with alien or foreign energy spirit personalities. Attack people that are asleep and/or trying to rest, are also (surprisingly) effected by these hotels and even some truck stop environments, where some RV customers (spirit energies that have attached to them – meaning these people willingly house these energies, and the people seem to be devoted to the energetic causes, or some call it ignorance) can be found engaging certain customers, trying to find rest at their facility, seem to think they need to energetically spirit-force people (that have paid for their services; food and/or gas, etc.,) out. O yea, it gets real out here. Just trying to stay out of others *spiritually contaminated spaces* can take *all day but you may only have 5 hours to get some serious sleep!* Then these businesses sometimes will call the police to help scare the people out. But often the person does not necessarily realize what is going on (other than having to deal suddenly with excess spirit energy activity aimed at them and they just want to sleep). Excess energy activity in the environment has to come from a source – Acts 19.16, which is becoming a learned behavioral community response. Actually often happens to the guest and becomes a development. Seeing that the hotel and its workers are not really knowing how to make their environments more spiritually safe.

Often these hotel guests are being provoked by a work environment imagination that has or is being tampered with by the energetic beings of whom the hotel is adjusting to (beings that are territorial) intruding on the scene. So then police may say, "Well it's your right, it's your property." OK, but *it is for unjust (or innocent) situations and who is teaching or instructing otherwise*. Why should people seeking rest at the rest areas, seem to over-concern our officers. Officer, Officer, don't you make an issue out of people seeking rest at our parks in "your" territory also?

Why does it seem like its OK for everyone to give or pass their issues on to everyone else. Yet everyone else is expected to just keep up with the pace of life, carrying everyone else's spiritual issues that seem to becoming heavier and heavier? Then when someone gets pushed and pushed to the point they need grace and/or help to go on; everyone in certain positions to help, instead, offer no mercy. All we see is the ***accuser of the brethren.*** Rev. 12.10. The real concern is that had someone shown mercy to some who apparently needed help but no one gives it! This is the degree that these energetic spirit aliens activities have effected those who used to be more helpful and more of what we use to call "humanitarian." However, without resistance, people are truly beginning to take on the energetic spirit activities that are trying to manifest in their soul and lives. Mk. 9.21. Acts 19.15.

**Unjust activity in the earth seems to get God's attention.** Amos 5.15. Jere. 9. 6, 23-24. But when everything plays out, the bottom line is that people are revealing cultural offenses and/or attitudes. Truth be told, attitudes and offenses are really manifestations that are being brought to light by territorial energetic spirit beings <u>already</u> operating in the lives of those in the work and private communities, as well as hotel environments, who could not apparently stop these beings from attaching. Why can't we see the bigger picture? Mostly all hotel experiences are very similar! So who is really caring that anyone is staying focused on our highways until someone gets pressed beyond their human abilities and accidents happen? Didn't Paul say he was pressed beyond measure? Was he able to find compassion? 2Corin. 1.8.

Often, those energetically forced (or voluntarily allowing the spirit energies to take over their soul) can't seem to find help, other than be given meds, which the energies eventually find ways to work around, then what? We need to understand how else, or other ways, we can deal with these energetic spirit beings (besides working with them to help irritate others). They literally cause some to commit suicide and/or bring harm to others (including causing situations that force people, inhibit or become the cause of others who are trying to find rest) from people or environments with <u>energetic spirit hounding personalities!</u> And we just write them off as another statistic because who has time to care? Who has time to deal with it? Who is being trained to care? What is wrong with this picture? Why do we only want to deal with the symptoms but not the issue that is causing the majority of society's ills? **Why** do we want to send our children to the moon **without** having to realize they may have to deal with wayward alien energetic spirit activities? What spiritual intelligence is in this? Why should it be a secret that these energetic beings can be dealt with in Jesus name because God has not given us the spirit of fear but of power and a sound mind! 2Tim 1.7. Why does it seem that most only think they can deal with a Holy God, (who is a Spirit) but not with other lesser intelligent beings to some effectiveness? Why do we allow our ignorance, often educational ignorance, to get in the way of who God may be directing to help bring healing answers and often, we are even kept from this level of spiritual consideration! Ignorance is a choice and/or comes by deception. Corin. 14.38. Mt. 22.29. Job 21.14. Either way someone is participating with the deception.

Why are we continually allowing our nation to be energetically victimized by ill-spirited means and/or by those these beings have victimized, one person at a time? With a little research we can find whistle blowers that have stated that these energetic spirit beings are the cause of making **America mental!**

<u>Las Vegas, NV comes to the forefront of our news community.</u>

Isn't Lakeisha Holloway found to be, or should I say, <u>*just as much*</u> as a victim as those who were harmed by temporary impairment? No one seemed to question, **nor be concerned,** that the reason Lakeisha was tired was due to a *broken* security system *found to be **uncompassionate** toward a homeless mother and child that lead up to the accident*. A homeless <u>*mother*</u> just needed sleep! Why would not this concern anyone?

"… for he shall have judgment without mercy that hath showed no mercy …"
James 2.10, 13-16.

- There is also a need for families and/or churches to gain the ability to effectively help those individuals being driven out from their familiar places. Seriously it is not always about YOU! If darkness is effectively protecting their work of darkness (among us), how much more the children of "light," <u>and we are the ones with the expected end!</u> Some of us first need to get spiritually released from some of the excess energy darkness is handing out. If you release yourself according to ***"The Spiritual Root of the Matter is Found in Me"***, perhaps then we can get enough of the light of Christ through His word to gain the ability to see and even help those among us, especially the household of faith. Please and thank you! Jere. 29.11. God does <u>not</u> set Himself out to help the wicked (like that which I am seeing). Helping someone who needs deliverance from darkness is not the same as helping those in darkness help others suffer and be unkind to the children of light. Please learn the difference. Allowing someone to use your body to help others manifest dark powers is not a Christian "duty". Then you go to church and want to mingle with the saints. Well so does the dark energy that you picked up at work! Yeah! I guess if I don't say this, who will? God is not the one bringing the confusion to your table. Who is sitting at your table? Corin. 14.33.

"Do not set foot on the path of the wicked …" Prov. 4.14.
"Blessed is the one who does not walk in the counsel of the wicked. "
Ps 1.1

Then highway deaths are pronounced on highway bulletins daily, reminding us to stay focused on driving. Yet we have men with "broken" security jobs and some spiritually effected police positions **who would rather harass and/or not be helpful to** homeless mothers or whoever is in need. They do not yet know how to release their souls from negative energetic intrusions evidently. Darkness is a monkey see, monkey do type of energy manifestation. Therefore, no one thinks twice about their behavior because everyone acts like them in a spiritually effected environment, rather than care about highway safety! We have hotel environments that do not promote "safe" sleep places and **even** <u>contribute</u> to unsafe sleep environments, regardless whether management realizes the energetic spirit issues concerning their hotels or not. Involving those who pay for a good nights sleep, who are suddenly awakened by some soul in the next room. Who doesn't know how to deal

**with their** excessive energetic spirit activity, who **are allowed** on their property to force out paid guests as well as policemen who monitor rest areas by camera or satellite – to do what, interrupt the people needing rest because they feel people are loitering in their territory! I am sorry we need to deal with these growing issues and concerns engaging us. Again, revealing their need for prayer and other necessary help. Seems like the highway bulletins are saying people are not getting their rest. So now are we trying to interpret statistically, what traffic accidents are being caused by tiredness because people can't find rest in our hotels nor rest areas? **Who** then is really caring about highway safety <u>more than</u> making sure <u>their territory</u> is not effected with "people issues and concerns" of what is really happening and being created among us? **No one wants to admit how** their non-caring ways are effecting or hindering those in need of sleep. Much is due to excessive energetic spirit influences (that showcase the same behavior whether in the body operating or in the atmosphere) that has and is bringing daily collisions and human catastrophes to a new time high. Did anyone mention that Lakeisha Holloway is a Christian? These are just some of the ways those with effected dark souls are attacking and pointing the finger at (or should I just say ways they <u>try not</u> to help) the Christians. Yet, we don't want to seem to connect the dots or look at the bigger picture! Why do the Christians have to continually suffer from or by those who just don't want to care how they effect others. Because they can say they have a degree in everything else but the Bible. This seems to mean they don't have to care, just keep them Christians out of our territory is what is really happening among us because our souls are in need of healing release!?

We are dealing with the same energetic intrusions that caused our army <u>to seal off AREA 51</u>! These same, often violent-natured, energetic beings (Acts 19.16) are able to cause the various community confusions and disharmony among us. These can also be reasons that Americans as well as other national communities need to learn how to release their souls from negative energies that want to attach and to express themselves negatively through souls and positions of men. Such as:

    – a night police car chase found 2 people dead after 137 rounds of ammunition, when an officer stood on the hood of the suspects car firing at least 15 shots into the suspects windshield. <u>www.clevelandcarchaseendswith2dead.com</u>

    – beings that are *able to pull people into sleep states while driving* and make it seem like it was the individual's problem alone.

    – beings that are able to pull a cars engine that is going around 60-70 mph down to 35 mph range, causing other drivers and police to think it's the drivers problem alone!

This is and has been done to cause people to notice and then call police, in order to get the police involved. All energetically instigated by these beings trying to pull a *person of their choice out of community,* seriously! It's how they can and do spiritually energetically attack to effect our physical world. They pull people away from the familiar, away from support systems then use men in authority, positioned among us to accuse their target further. This is Bible 101. Rev.12.9-11). Then these beings are able to take over the body and cause them to act out of character. This is the common denominator of these serious catastrophes happening among us including the causes behind:

- The Sandy Hook Elementary School shooting
- The Boston Marathon bombing

- The San Bernardino, CA shooting of 14 (these are all dark spiritual kingdom activities people; people processed by darkness to destroy … Jn 10.10.)

- also from the pictures included in this writing, these beings are also quite capable of destroying property while making it seem like the targeted person is the concern. This is why I say log what is energetically/spiritually happening to you. to show there is a mysterious pattern of energetic spirited disharmony trying to be a reality activity concerning you and needs to be recognized and dealt with appropriately. *Ignoring spiritual energetic disharmonious activity does not work for us.* It tends to create and allow for more disharmony and energetic spirit intrusion to breed while aiming against our various cultures, communities, market places and society at large.

- Yes, even ex. President, Tim Wolfe, *wherever* there is a struggle to do what is considered biblically right over those you reside. Here was/is a spiritual struggle that manifested in the natural/physical circumstances, as they all do eventually. This is also a good example where an individual struggle effects us all. Everyone is hurting people! Let's learn to recognize those being effected often different ways from others, but nevertheless, and this is why we pray, pray, pray and pray for the Lord's counsel and intervention continually for everyone, in Jesus name! *1Tim 2.11. As we can see negative energetic spirit realities can operate like a spreading social disease among us and is why men should always pray and not to faint.* 2Chr 23.6.

Luke 8.17. says for nothing is secret, that shall not be made manifest, neither anything hid, that shall not be known and come abroad (KJV).

***You don't have to be mental to deal with mental issues being created among us and/ or that are engaging us!*** We simply need to gain the ability to understand what we are dealing with *and deal with it in God's ability*. We don't need to keep blaming everything on others that are being victimized (spiritually and naturally so by those spiritually effected) because they are not able to get the help they need! We, believers in faith in Christ, it appears did not have a voice during our scientist decision to make a treaty with energetic alien spirit beings. Now, *are we still revealing that we do not have a prophetic voice in the police force* (where is the fruit), someone with understanding of spiritual kingdom activity? Please community of faith, remember our righteous officers of faith trying to do right, seemingly caught up in this seemingly spiritual mix. 1Tim. 2.1. Mt. 7.16.

### *How are you going to fight in an army or fight a battle that you cannot discern?* *Proverbs 3.21.*

Policemen and security men, who are supposed to be trained to protect us, are often found TOO energetically spirit effected and are found (as the news has been revealing) to have become UNSAFE PLACES FOR US! We just seem to need more **"light"** in our police force so we can see more clearly how to overcome the work and operation of darkness happening among us because light **excels** darkness. Ecc. 2.13. Job 29.3.

OK! So, can we just learn to deal and engage that which evidently is engaging us, please? Can we just learn to deal with the elephant in the room and stop stepping or tripping over it, please?

Maybe we think we are dealing with the energetic spirit intrusions acceptably (as NASA and those involved with the Gennady Treaty). Our society has, and continues to be backed up by the excess energy activity from other planets. A sort of energetic constitutional and societal constipation has, and continues to occur due to our looking the other way or blame shifting (and/or letting come what may) to what these energetic alien excess spirit activities are causing among us, just to sustain their species while destroying ours! Can we realize that if an Area 51 can be created for experimental purposes that went wrong, then it should not be a stretch that these energetic beings are creating other types of disharmonious <u>territorial</u> area 51's in our communities and nation? Where they are found "acting out disharmoniously" among us, whether in our environments and/or through those effected by them is not hidden! Lk. 8.17.

It continues to be apparent that our society, our nation as well as other nations, and its inhabitants need to understand that we are being forced to coexist with other worldly energetic spirit beings. Like Robin Williams, as an example, needed to be retrained and taught how to deal with initially visiting spirit beings and/or how to coexist with or resist if necessary, other worldly energetic spirit beings such as:

> - know when one is being put in danger by any consistent spirit energy visitations
>
> - how to recognize what symptoms they can cause so we can off-set it immediately instead of waiting until the symptoms become to be unbearable. So we as a society don't drop like flies, nor be consumed in whatever generation these beings <u>decide</u> to show up in.

That we as a society can gain the ability, as a family, people, community and nation, to learn how to maintain our souls and how to function if spiritually challenged. Then we are more than bodies walking around, people!

Our nation and those in our society that took part in being silent when the alien energetic spirit beings breached their agreement with NASA should have opened their mouth to warn our society and teach us how to protect ourselves from these types of spiritual breaches because the "silence" did and does not work for us! Jesus, Himself said:

# My People Perish for Lack of Knowledge

Hosea 4.6.

It was the intrusion of the energetic spirit beings that were able to, obviously, operate and/or even take the place of many in our society, that taught our society how to be silent (and just let them do what they are doing among us). From this we can also learn that being too spiritually effected can and has harmed us. Why spiritual release is sometimes needed, not just for the few but for all (or anyone who can potentially be effected by them), as well as cost the lives of those at home, more than the lives lost in wars battled against other nations. In other words, it is an alien energetic spirit inside job (that was allowed by our nation, through NASA, to observe us) not only effecting us, but now operating among us, teaching us (who they can, that is whoever else they are effecting) to be like them, and oppose those who are not or not willing to be like them. These energetic spirit beings are literally teaching us how to war against another (like in Lakeisha Holloway's case), by the segments of our society literally being attacked (these beings have become and/or the influenced in our society and communities). In this sense everyone (or even segments of society are left to fend for themselves). In this respect, we have allowed these energetic spirit beings to literally split up our society, as well as families, the way they are attacking us. As Paul said, warring's within and without! Ecc.3.7.

And as it has been said before, where is our spiritual intelligence (knowledge and understanding of spiritual things). It is difficult to discern what one has become a part of is what some of us have done to self preserve. OK, but how does or did that work overall for others or for the next generation?

## Example 8

Then on Wednesday, December 23, 2015, *I thought I was done with this writing*. After work, I went to buy a fish sandwich and ice cream. I then went to the **rest area** by the University Hospital, I-90 on the west side of the highway around exit number 200. I pulled into the rest area and began to eat my sandwich. Around 15 minutes later I happened to look up, or so I thought, only to find 2 police cars, one behind the other, parked along side the island that divides the rest area drivers from the truck drivers. At first glance in my rear view mirror, I just assumed these officers were just passing through. However after some time, I just began to sense and feel like there was darkness arousing itself around me, literally directed in my direction by these 2 officers, but why, I thought. Why, did not seem to be the police issues these days only, its just what they are doing (being led as Paul said). Corin. 12.2.

It seemed apparent, these officers were giving me their attention and with all of the attention that officers and certain questionable behaviors, I suppose like the one I was currently experiencing. I thought it best to move on than get pulled into these officers reality, that seemed to have little to do with me, than what their imaginations were manifesting. As I moved on, I felt a bit discouraged that after work it was still a beautiful Christmas Eve day, being evidently cut off by those apparently spiritually energetically effected (there is no other explanations for these types of behavior happening among us people!). I continued on, looking for a peaceful place or harmonious environment (other than the environment effected by the territorial environment the officers were at) to eat. Surely its not illegal to eat at the rest areas? Or was it illegal to enjoy a beautiful day! Some nights when you can't sleep, you can literally catch some officers suddenly park and stare at some people in their vehicles, until they release the energy operating in their life (causing them to do this) until they actually disturb someone's rest, then they move on! Again, people's civil rights are violated, whether at the rest areas, hotels or whatever parking lot one feels they need to find to get the needed sleep! And yes, this is a bigger issue happening among us.

Anyway, as I finished eating at another location, I found my mind going back to what these officers were doing (or so I thought it was me).

Until suddenly, I began to sense and feel a warning in my spirit. I found myself sensing a type of state of alarm, because many of our officers have become and the word that came to me was "unfit." The conversation I somehow began to pick up continued. Any officer with an alienist view of those he is supposed to protect has become "unfit," STL (says the Lord). Then I shook myself thinking, I must be really tired. Then I found myself distinguishing the following 2 terms:

| **Alienist** | **Unfit** |
|---|---|
| One whose views are uncomparably different; Other worldly beings contrary to your created purpose.  Rom. 16.17. Gal 1.8 | Can be defined as unhealthy; Inappropriate |
| (not the same term used by a psychiatrist who specializes in aspects of mental illness) | Inadequate, no longer operating for their intended purpose |

(then the analysis came to me that, for the most part, not adapted to the spiritual trouble that has engaged them) They, for the most part, continue to show signs of being spiritually overcome.

Rom. 12.21.  2 Pet 2.19.

---

Then I began to get strategy, all this information just continued to stream into my soul as if I had asked for it, but I didn't.

# As I looked, watched and listened I began to
Prov. 19.21.

observe what was passing before my eyes! I began to see Pastors opening up their properties to those in need of rest, read, study and/or perhaps simply a safe place to think and/or sleep, etc.

I saw this would, and could, also speak to other "needs" or concerns. As I could also see Pastors (whomever the Lord is speaking to), able to even take a reasonable fee to help maintain the area and/or give grace, where needed, with the priority being a safe place and/or place of refugee!

There are a variety of ways to collect fees, such as:

> By the day,
> By the hour or
> Monthly; simply seek the Lord for your situation.

Once you become available, you will be able to find someone to help those who come seeking a safe place and/or a place to rest, even a place to praise, (using ear phone) in their hearts to the Lord (not looking for obligations … rest!) Hopefully someone who can potentially gain the ability, and be mindful, to release themselves from excessive or wayward spirit energies, their attachments and tactics! In Jesus name. Amen. Amen.

I saw where a place was available in your services – to announce and/or even a community (perhaps internet, radio, TV, etc.), PSA announcing that your parking lot property is available for those needing a **safe place** in community to rest. Please give hours and location and anything else that that may be relevant.

There is a need to keep those being targeted (such ways as we have seen in the news) so far those of darker cultures and/or women, with or without children, *off and out of our streets, rest areas, truck stops. Drivers in their vehicles, and many found in security services, even cart collectors at local stores in parking lots can be found secretly trying to discern those of light (though they learn it as energies not like theirs). They can be found trying to call police to remove certain people in lots for absurd reasons, etc.* Whatever else becomes the issue of places and absurd reasons to attack, these who also seek safe places from the Lord. We no longer see the needs of people but have learned to see them as inconveniences *in our territories!* I continued listening in this place and then I heard:

Until our **officers and businesses of concern** displaying these "absurd indifferences and and/other unwarranted spiritual hostilities" and are able to deal with the matters and causes of concern of their growing absurd indifferences, being privately and publically expressed towards those of different cultures and/or certain genders among us effecting the above (but not only) mentioned places found in our cities, communities and marketplaces of ideas.

– Absurd defined as: often inappropriate, illogical, and wildly unreasonable.

-Synonyms for absurd: preposterous, ridiculous, ludicrous, farcical, laughable, idiotic, stupid, foolish, silly, harebrained, cockamamie. This is what darkness is trying to bring to our table, the table that the Lord is preparing for us in the presence of our enemies! O yea, taste and see that the Lord is good! Ps. 23.5. Ps. 34.8. Somebody give me an Amen!

For those who need to drive alone: Please log any and all noticeable police interaction and/or any community businesses or marketplaces (colleges, universities, truck stops, security services, etc.,) expressing any of the above mentioned indifferences – where police comes on the scene. Please make weekly and/or monthly copies and give to the Pastor where you may normally go to church, places of refuge and/or safe places. Especially if for the reasons above you are often found looking for safe places. Pastors can designate these documents to be filed by first and last name,

We need to recognize and know the difference of maintaining oneself in the Bible ways expressed in God's kingdom versus operating for darkness (as a spiritual force that is not right nor acceptable to us from God Almighty's perspective).

## Kingdom of God & His Operation

(no matter the religion, in this kingdom righteousness prevails)

## Operation of darkness

(no matter the religion it is converted into dark works)

### Both have spiritual directives

*One causes and helps you to be still before the Lord as we praise, meditate and study His word*

*This one usually comes by, or through, an intrusion that it is able to eventually create in your spirit life, soul and body.*

*Whose presence comes in peaceful ways when we seek Him in prayer, praise, and sometimes when we study … Amen*

*Usually comes with a different, dark manifestation that comes in or upon the physical body (usually unwarranted intruding ways), causing some type of physical discomfort and is a reason they struggle being still, calm*

Respect others, and civil rights of others

This category of study violates the rights of others through energetic spirit acts and often emotionalism prevails here.

Fruit of God's Spirit love, joy, peace, gentleness … etc

Gal 5.13,17-22

Excessive emotions, of which usually sound scripture emotions, not just any emotions. This category supports spirit domination, perversion, often rudeness. Often when one comes to Christ, one can learn to release any negative emotions through the authority of God's word, grace and love. **The Spiritual Root of the Matter is Found in Me** can be found to help in areas of needing release in Jesus.

Scripture always points to light and truth! Godly emotions usually supported and embraced in truth of God's word, light.

Bible teaches God's people to teach between the holy and profane things … Eze. 44.23 (Then shall the righteous shine forth as the sun in the Kingdom of their Father … Mt. 13.43)

Due to the spiritual confusion and disruptions that the operations of darkness has and continues to try to operate among us, Churches (and Christian based facilities) make sure that your leaders can be still before the Lord, can praise and study before the Lord. If not, make time for the Lord in these areas not because they "just got-ta" but because they are grateful to the Lord and love Him, because He created us, we are not trying to create Him. There are many ways to abide with the Lord and Israel has always been an abiding, and being still before the Lord is also biblically viewed as abiding according to Numbers 24.2:

And Balaam lifted up his eyes and saw Israel abiding …

If any of your leaders are manifesting and/or using other dark spirited expressions (perhaps due to the excessive energy activities surrounding us), then they will need to learn how to not manifest (or resist the various manifestations according to James 4.7.) and with the sprays and/or creams (when needed) listed in this writing (or whatever ways that work that the Lord may reveal to you we are free in Christ). Also how to biblically release themselves according to the method's listed in _The Spiritual Root of the Matter is Found in Me_ can prove helpful, thank you Lord. If there are police who are leaders and/or laymen in the Church, they need to know and understand the ways of the Lord. That energetically the ways and expression(s) of the Lord are not the same as the operation of darkness whereby you just let any and all energetic spirit activity come upon you, to do anything it wants to make and cause you to be dumb like them. Mark 9.25. If the leaders can't be still before the Lord, then how can they teach it? We can recall the story of Martha and Mary where Mary sat at the Lord's feet and Martha was seemingly always distracted … Lk 10.38-42. Ps. 46.10 says:

# Be Still and Know that I AM **God**

Get it. Got it. Good!

Simply because we are all called to be civil, civilized and those who struggle in these areas simply and obviously, need to learn how to use _Bible energy_ and engage and resist that which is evidently causing one not to be civil or be restful towards another.

> We biblically recognize that God's love and kingdom welcomes all cultures, therefore, any cultures needing safe places, rest places, are welcome to the churches that are able and that announce as such. Rom. 10.12.

Learning to maintain one's soul unto the Lord is for all men and women, not just believers, even for those who have been deceived by darkness. How else could anyone learn how to protect their soul which is also a process of maintaining one's soul from darkness, trying to take over men and turn them into beasts and/or until they are "unfit" because all beasts do is fight to survive. Currently, it may seem like men, those spiritually effected are trying to create a territory to survive in and are revealing among us those they evidently are not wanting in their territory. How sad that darkness can cause some men to live such a limited and limiting life. Men allowing themselves to be bound in the territories, using cords of hate, and afflicting and dividing others to get there. This is what darkness is teaching them how to create among us. Job 36.8. Does this sound like America the free?

To Pastors able to make parking available, please note: If one person pulls up to or beside another and if the person that pulls up causes an unrest, due to the person's energy, trying to operate through the person that just pulled up. It is OK. The person that pulled up should perhaps move a couple rows back or away from the person (or wherever it is safer) that was already there, until the initial person's peace is restored. Now we are able to make a better distinction between those with seemingly restless spirit activity and/or those at peace and/or perhaps needing less noticeable releases. Also, when people are being engaged with what may seem like body heat manifestations, which can be handled with water in a small or medium size spray bottle with water. Some may get a better response to releases from these types of sudden body heat by adding some peppermint (extract spray) found at local grocery stores. It is, however, very important <u>not</u> to let people manifest heat and do nothing because these heat manifestations (or negative energy) can release and attach to whoever is near and cause distress. So, to keep everyone safe, respect one another's space, please.

On December 24th, 2015 after recording the above spiritual downloads or revelations of the Lord, I fell asleep early, wondering about the timing of the above information and if that was all that was needed for this writing because I did need to get this book to the publisher, around 11-12mid.

Well, I awoke around 3 a.m. on Christmas day thinking that I needed to go back to sleep. Suddenly, again my sleep thoughts were interrupted regarding our policemen – how it seemed like the enemy was trying to use them, while simultaneously removing humanity from our humanity.

# PROCLAMATION

Then suddenly, I could hear myself in God saying:

> Mr. Officer. Mr. Officer, you need to learn how to deal with your energies. Get up and deal with it and stop allowing it (the excess alien energies) to come through YOU!

Then I heard the word of the Lord for our officers, in a type of authority from on high that the policeman can understand and I heard the Lord say aloud (as if He wanted you to hear Him from heaven)

# "Sit Down -
# And MOVE OUT OF THE WAY!"

**SAYETH THE LORD**

**And I heard the Lord say,**

> Humble yourselves in the sight of the Lord and He will lift you up in due season!  Pet 5.6

There is a need for you to learn how to deal with excess energies.

There is a need for you to find a church that understands how to deal with excess negative alien spirit energies.

Churches, this is also an opportune time to come along side of our Officers. **They cannot heal with you sayeth the Spirit of Your Father!**

Then, I heard

## I have spoken, sayeth the Lord

Jere.23.28

_____

Now, I better understand why my spiritual warfare was seemingly so difficult, I'm carrying a word for the nation! O merciful Savior as the former prophets have said, do not leave us, we are still in need of You, Lord! Arise Oh Lord among us in your glory, honor, power and majesty! As I say this in my heart, I can still see the heavens close, wishing they'd never close, as they had opened for our sake.

## *Happy Birthday, Lord Jesus!*

We thank You for grace. We bless Your name. We thank You for all things, and may the Lord confirm this word, His grace, in Jesus name. Amen and Amen. Isa. 44.26. Heb. 2.4. Mk. 16.20. Acts 14.3.

---

*We will wait on the Lord.* **This is the Lord's Watch!** Ps. 121.5.Prov. 15.3.Ps. 121.5-3. Ps. 121. Ps.130.5. Ps. 27.14. Ps. 37.34.

# Book References

King James Bible, KJV.

The Secret Life, David Jacobs, PH.D, Fireside Publishing, Copyright, 1995

The Threat, David Jacobs, PH.D,

The Dark Side of Cupid, by Eve Lorgen

DVDs
Ancient Aliens, Season 6, Vol. 2. 3 disc.; History Channel; where One of the commentators said that he did not agree with alien agenda, Produced by Prometheus Entertainment for H2, 2013-2014.

Area 51.com
UnawareDVD.com

QuWave.com; products are geared toward protecting your energy field and overall well-being. Sincere praise and laughter can also bring healing and protection to your energy field and over all well-being! Proverbs 17.22. Exo. 15.11. 2Sam. 22.4. 1Chr. 16.25; 34-36. Please remember that Praise and laughter are also healing! Prov. 17.22. 3Jn. 1-2. Prov. 3.7-8. Ps. 23.25.

Try: Exercise DVD's for Abs.com; to help exercise, to help keep limbs active. Some DVD sessions, takes only 25 minutes a day!

Trampoline, any size is available for you and/your family needs.

---

*The books and other material listed here are noted for excellent research content.

# Other Relevant References Index

www.biggestsecret,doreptilitan-humanhybridsrunourworld.com:

> The ultimate measure of a man is not where he stands in moments of comfort and convenience, but where he stands at times of challenge and controversy.
> Martin Luther King

This website speaks of the Reptilian Hybrid controlling our world race and the dumbing down of the masses by pharmaceutical drugs and alcohol, etc. and mental America (or Reptilian domination in the marketplace and business). A must read!

www.blackopswhistleblowerexposesalientakeover.com: About the official policy of all governments to deny that the extra-terrestrial phenomenon exists. However, this is no longer possible due to:

- overwhelming amount of leaked documentation.

- credible high level testimony.

- genuine experiences and extensive research proving otherwise.

Our freedoms (our abilities to stay free) are depending on:

> - seeing and timing when we are truly up against insurmountable things operating against us.

### *Therefore, genuine whistle blowers are critical at the present time!*

This website is revealing agreements between the U.S. Government and extra-terrestrials giving the right to experiment on humans and cattle in exchange for technology, called the "Grenada Treaty."

After which began the alien human conflict, because aliens were found taking more humans than initially agreed to. Presently the USA, Russia and China can be found in constant conflict with aliens. It seems presently there are 11 different races of aliens in the earth. A must read!

*Author's Page*

# *Greetings in the name of the Lord!*

We have been observing churches since around 2000, 5 years prior to this time the Lord sent me through church boot camp. Since then, we have been literally brought into experiences that the church is dealing with, areas that the Lord is desiring to help His church with greater understanding and then the Lord releases me to write. In this way, the Lord connects any kingdom apostolic prophetic assignment we may be researching to the local church.

There was much learned in this battle. In this respect, this writing reaches out, in Jesus Name, seeking those who have tried or are still trying to find help from energetic spirit intrusions or otherworldly beings, help that may not be found in mainstream society. A changing society that maybe considered or has become too effected (even changed) by energetic alien spirit processes among us. From the most professional occupations among us to the least, no stone was unturned (or at some level effected). Alien operations of dark-ness have become the 21st century of dark crimes happening among us.

         And … while men slept (or were distracted, or you could say, were put to sleep) his enemy came. Mt 13.25.

This writing is not meant to replace any legitimate Doctor's care. You are free to share this information with any professional that you feel *has not been so energetically* spirit alien effected to where their judgment would be too compromised to benefit you. Surely a doctor could find even more possibilities other than what I have found helpful to work, with consistency, in this writing. Otherwise this writing could prove to be a beneficial supplemental aid to the unusual energetic alien operations happening among us. To hope-fully help bring more of a balanced (or removal to any imbalanced) energy trying to engage you with the ability to ritually cause sickness and/or disease.

Some learn how to effectively resist hostile spiritual energetic activity, concerning the saints of God. Some among us have been forcefully too energetically effected (spiritually) and have, thereby, been enlisted by alien energetic intentions to resist the saints among us (family or not … there are no demonic graces among the aliens).
Do you understand this?

Much of the information in this writing was the only way we found to keep myself free enough, to stay biblically sound enough to tell or suggest to others how to resist this type of alien battle happening among us!

A selective battle revealing that those who have submitted to alien agendas are doing less struggling than those who are still resisting, according to James 4.7. We have sensed the need to write this as an aid because some in the mainstream professions are too effected to help and the concern is that they have not yet realized it. Not everyone in our society or community is, or should be, considered crazy just because they have been pulled into the alien reality. They only need someone to teach them other ways (if medicines should fail) and/or other possibilities when dealing with invisible energetic activity that have the ability to paralyze a body, effect others mentally, or even cause others to think you are the issue when really they are and this is where the word can be helpful. Scripture and consistent communion with the Lord can literally help a person find their way when being plagued by darkness. I mean really, this is the 21$^{st}$ century! Especially when energies know how to work around any prescribed meds!

Can we learn how to pass on to our children "faith" in God over the alien's initiatives for the family, please? Study reveals that some professions have been uncovering alien intentions for over 50 years now. While the aliens have been using that time to find ways to fit into our society and cultures, pressing forward in their obvious attempt among us to overtake our society at **our expense**, one person at a time, one family at a time, one community at a time!

So what we are seeing and is going on among us is what the scientist wants to call our "benevolent space brothers – but research is actually revealing secret intrusive energetic activity and a hostile agenda going on," is now manifesting among us. Scripture reveals that there is nothing hidden that shall not be revealed. Mt 10.26., Mk 4.22.

We can also learn from study that our alien space brothers in disguise (any human disguise is the issue here) have the ability to cause those they abduct to begin to befriend them. Also through a process of releasing their energy (or spiritual penetration/and mind scan exercises) into/or concerning their human subject by way of daily, nightly, or 24/7 if subject chooses to resist their intentions. This then, turns out to be ritualistic visitations with no one in society to really listen, without the urge to put the person away and/or claim them to be mental. So the subject learns to resist by cleaving, crying and praying to the Lord while feeling alone simply because the alien has the ability to either work through any health profession that has been affected to the demise or degree of the alien's subject, and again, another reason for this writing, in Jesus Name! Those who resist can be found dealing with any, but not limited to, the symptoms listed in this writing. Kind of threatening isn't it? This occurs until the human subject becomes overcome by the alien's energy activity. Many have become statistics among us and many have died because the alien knows how to work around any medication. So we really need to understand how the enemy is gaining entrance into the body and how to resist physically in case an alternative is needed!

# *Photo Pages*

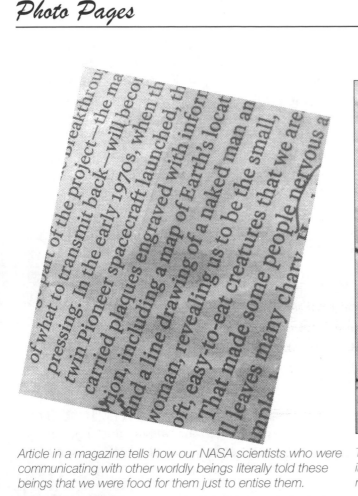

*Article in a magazine tells how our NASA scientists who were communicating with other worldly beings literally told these beings that we were food for them just to entise them.*

*Perhaps we should have our scientists take psychological tests to prevent or give other beings reasons to visit us as their resource for food (at our expense).*

*These colored plaques are how these other worldly beings intruded into my life so freely as if I had called them but I did not – we were all being observed.*

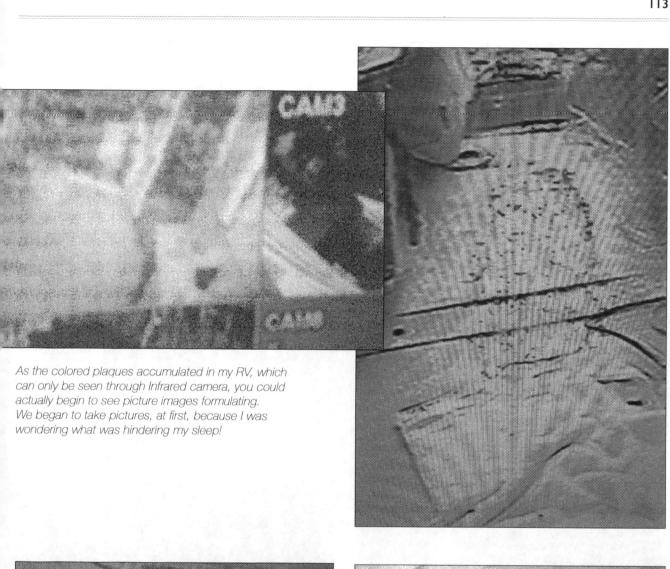

As the colored plaques accumulated in my RV, which can only be seen through Infrared camera, you could actually begin to see picture images formulating. We began to take pictures, at first, because I was wondering what was hindering my sleep!

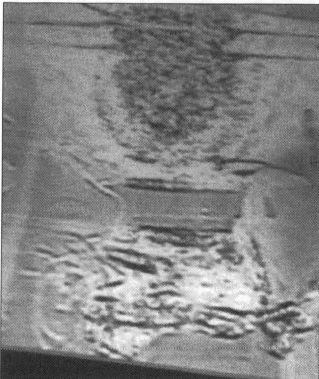

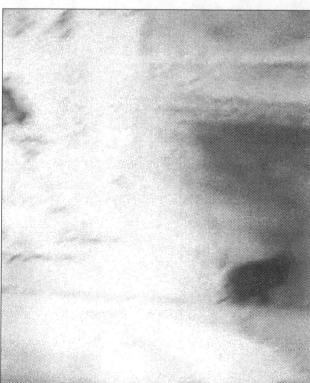

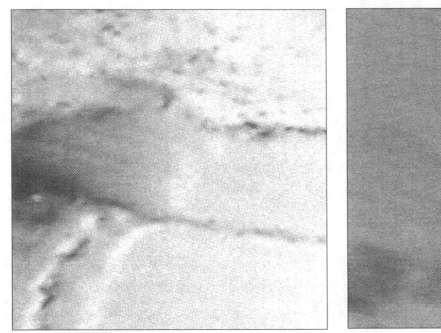

*When the energetic spirit being saw that we were recording what they were trying to do to my immediate environment (RV), they (energetic spirit beings) began to immediately erase my evidence but it was too late.*

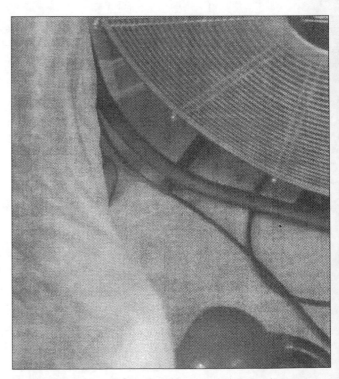

*Here, as the energy was being erased or washed away, you could see me sleeping. You could only see this activity (spirit energy activity) by infrared camera.*

*In this same manner, officers and those in store security – not just Walmart but Staples are affected, when they stare into the camera for a lengthy time. The negative energies they*

*are connected to will flow thru the camera lens and cause a person to act out of character. (However, if one recognizes that this is happening.) In my next book (Spiritual Recovery) I reveal the purifier one can drink to stop this type of spirit energy abuse!*

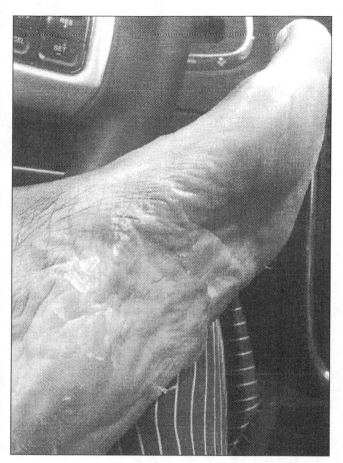

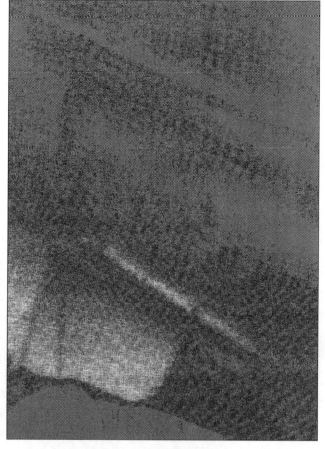

*Energy spirit activity in the feet area can cause redness, soreness, chapping, or peeling skin issues. So I wrapped my feet in paper towels to keep them dry then I would change the foot padding when it got wet, to interrupt the energies intent in this area.*

*Some of the unmarked vehicles can look like this. These particular vehicles used by law enforcement at any particular Walmart store, when called it seemingly and whenever a darker cultured person would come on the stores' property. Somes darker cultures were under "energetically spirit types of attack," even before they could get out of their vehicles. There is no seemingly other verbal communication (no reasons asked) only assumed to remove the darker cultures so often darker cultures acting strange at times, caught on camera, was due to someone in law enforcement and/ or security using negative concentrated spirit energy to discomfort the darker culture way to cause them to act out of character – to get it on camera just to reveal the targeted darker cultures is issue. However, it is really the law enforcer causing the ill behavior's issue.*

## *Notes*

Printed in the United States
By Bookmasters